# UNCHAINED
# LEADERSHIP

**EDWARD E. ACKAH-NYAMIKE JNR.(Ph.D)**

*ISBN: 978-9988-2-3665-6 (Paperback)*
*ISBN: 978-9988-2-3666-3 (e-book)*


*For enquiries contact the author on:*
*email- eackah9@gmail.com*


**Design & Print**
*Print Innovation*
*+233 267 771 670 / 020 2014 893*

*www.print-innovation.com*

### The Man in the Arena

*"It is not the critic who counts; not the man who points out how the strong man stumbles, or where the doer of deeds could have done them better.  The credit belongs to the man who is actually in the arena, whose face is marred by dust and sweat and blood; who strives valiantly; who errs, who comes short again and again, because there is no effort without error and shortcoming; but who does actually strive to do the deeds; who knows great enthusiasms, the great devotions; who spends himself in a worthy cause; who at the best knows in the end the triumph of high achievement, and who at the worst, if he fails, at least fails while daring greatly, so that his place shall never be with those cold and timid souls who neither know victory nor defeat."*

Excerpt from the Speech "Citizenship in a Republic" delivered by Theodore Roosevelt at Sorbonne in Paris, France 23rd April, 1910.

To my "Pentateuch": Derrick; Kojo; Yaba; Akasi; and Immanuel. May God use you mightily in various leadership positions according to His will.

# CONTENTS

## ACKNOWLEDGMENTS

I received inspiration and various support from the following individuals and groups in the build up to the publication of this book:

- ❖ Mrs. Juliet Ackah-Nyamike, my beloved wife.
- ❖ Ackah-Nyamike Family: my mum, Mrs. Veronica Ackah-Nyamike; my sisters, Mrs Antonia Bediako and Mrs. Patricia Danso Abiam; and my brother Brighte Ackah-Nyamike.
- ❖ Members of Ackah-Eyepa Abozoama: Kabla-Degnan siblings; Ackah-Nyamike siblings; Ackah-Nyanzu siblings.
- ❖ Mr. Kofi Akpabli, a journalist and lecturer in communication at Central University.
- ❖ Print Innovation, publishers of the book.
- ❖ Management and Staff of Venaco Lodge Ltd.
- ❖ Executives and members of Ghana Hotels Association, especially Greater Accra Regional Branch.
- ❖ Executives and members of Beautifulgate Chapter of Full Gospel Business Men's

Fellowship International.

❖ Executives and members of APSU '84 (1984 Year Group of St. Augustine's College Past Students Union).

❖ Madam Elizabeth Owusu (Director of Acacia Lodge, with branches at Haatso and North Kaneshie).

❖ Staff and students of Department of Agricultural Extension, University of Ghana, Legon (1996 – 2009).

God richly bless you all.

# PREFACE

One of the questions that became all too familiar to me after the launch of my midlife autobiography in November 2012 was, "..so when is your next book coming up'? My response was consistent: "As the Holy Spirit directs". And indeed I believe the Holy Spirit graciously directed me to write this book on leadership.

As was the case in the writing of my midlife story, I also received a firm confirmation to write this book. I recollect meeting Apostle George Gadri a Pastor brother of my lady friend, Gifty Gadri, for the first time at their mum's funeral in 2013 He is resident in the United States and had travelled to Ghana purposely to participate in the burial and funeral services of his dear mum. Apparently, he had gleaned through my midlife autobiography on arrival and had expressed interest in meeting me. When we met at the funeral grounds he prophesied, after exchange of pleasantries, that my next book was going to be on leadership. I received the prophecy in Jesus' mighty name and glorified God for the direction.

In the days and months that followed the prophecy, I suddenly became extra conscious of my leadership experiences and roles, as well as my passion for effective leadership. Subsequently, I jotted a number of points down and that set the ball rolling for the writing of this book. My objective for writing this book was very clear from the beginning: to inspire more people into leadership positions by making the topic of leadership easier to understand and more practical. I trust that you shall be greatly inspired after reading this book to take up a leadership position or perform your leadership role more effectively to the glory of God.

# CHAPTER ONE

## THE GENESIS OF LEADERSHIP

"In the beginning God created the heaven and the earth" (Genesis 1:1), and went on to create man "in His own image......male and female" (Genesis 1:27). According to the Bible, God blessed them and said unto them "Be fruitful, and multiply, and replenish the earth, and subdue it: and have dominion over the fish of the sea, and over the fowl of the air, and over every living thing that moveth upon the earth" (Genesis 1:28). With this mandate, according to the Christian Faith, man started his existence on earth, passing through various periods such as the Paleolithic Era (Early Stone Age), Neolithic Era (New Stone Age), Agricultural Revolution, Middle ages and Scientific Revolution to the present technology age.

One major characteristic of man's existence across the various historical eras is the fact that man is a social being – we live and operate in groups i.e. families,

1

communities, societies, associations, corporate organisations etc. Groups, irrespective of their composition, grow by continuously addressing their needs, aspirations, problems and/or challenges. This calls for leadership, that is, the provision of guidance, support and inspiration by a person(s) to the group to enable the group address its problems, challenges, needs and/or aspirations.

Historical and Biblical narrations are replete with leaders who excelled in their leadership roles and provided some blue prints for effective leadership. For the purpose of this book, I present below the classical leadership stories of Moses and Alexander the Great to give a glimpse of what effective leadership is all about.

The guidance, support, and inspiration provided by Moses to the Israelites in their exodus from Egypt to the Promised Land is one of the classical examples of leadership that has been studied over and over again. According to the Bible, Moses was born to Levite parents after Pharaoh decreed the death of all new born Hebrew boys. To probably escape the decree, Moses' mother set him in a shallow part of the Nile River where he was discovered by Pharaoh's daughter. As fate would have it, the Princess raised

Moses as her son, employing Moses' natural mother as his nurse.

In his early manhood Moses began to explore life outside the palace. Coming upon a fight between an Egyptian and a Hebrew he killed the Egyptian and hid the body. When he later interrupted a fight between two Hebrews his previous homicide was thrown at him and he fled to Midian. In Midian, Moses encountered the daughters of the local priest, Jethro, who welcomed him into his household and gave him his daughter, Zipporah, in marriage.

Sometime later, while tending sheep, Moses encountered the Almighty God in a burning bush. God revealed to Moses His true name, Yahweh, and reaffirmed His ancient promise to bring Israel to Canaan. Overruling Moses' repeated objections, God sent him back to Egypt to deliver Israel, assisted by his brother Aaron and armed with the rod of God.

After delivering God's word to the joyous people, Moses confronted Pharaoh. But the king only made Israel's suffering harsher, sowing dissent among the Israelites. Moses was dismayed but God reiterated His promise to deliver Israel. God sent ten plaques against Egypt to force Pharaoh to allow the Israelites to leave. After the tenth plague, Pharaoh allowed the Israelites to leave.

After leading them to cross the Red Sea, Moses led them through the desert, miraculously providing water, quails, and manna; defeating the Amalekites and, with Jethro's guidance, establishing the Israelite Judiciary. Throughout, the Israelites complained against Moses but God continuously vindicated him. Finally they reached Sinai, where they camped for eleven months and entered into a covenant with God. Yahweh's covenant obligation was to give Israel prosperity in their own land and Israel's obligation was to worship Yahweh alone and to obey all His moral and ritual laws to be received by Moses atop Mount Sinai.

When Moses delayed in returning with the laws, Aaron built a golden calf for the Israelites to worship. On his return from the mountain, Moses smashed the tablets of the covenant and ordered all idolaters killed. God proposed to wipe out Israel and create a new nation out of Moses, but Moses declined the honour and placated God. A new covenant was enacted and Moses brought two new tablets down from the mountain. During this second revelation Moses had an almost direct experience of God.

Finally, after a census was taken, Israel set forth from Sinai, bearing the ritual tabernacle they had built to house Yahweh's presence. But the people's rebellion continued. Frustrated, Moses demanded more assistance from God who invested seventy prophets to help him. This led Aaron and Miriam, their sister, to question Moses's unique leadership. Moses declined to defend himself but Yahweh afflicted Miriam with temporary leprosy.

Subsequently Moses dispatched twelve spies to reconnoiter Canaan. When all the twelve but Caleb and Joshua reported that the land was impregnable, the Israelites refused to progress into the Promised Land and again wished they were back in Egypt. Moses once more dissuaded Yahweh from destroying Israel for their disobedience. However, Yahweh decreed that all the people, except Caleb and Joshua, shall not see the Promised Land. So, sadly, the Israelites turned back into the wilderness where they stayed for forty years. At some point during the forty years, a handful of the Israelites rebelled against Moses and Aaron, contesting their unique claim to religious office and blaming their apparent inability to bring Israel to Canaan. Yahweh killed all the rebels. Again the Israelites rebelled, demanding water. Yahweh instructed Moses to take Aaron's rod and address a rock to yield water. Moses struck the rock with the rod instead. The water gushed out alright but because of that disobedience both Moses and Aaron were condemned to die in the desert and thereby never stepping in Canaan.

At the end of the forty years in the wilderness, Israel was back at Kadesh preparing to enter the Promised Land. When they embarked on the conquest, various nations tried to stop them but the Israelites strategically avoided some and defeated others. During this time Moses averted a plaque of fiery serpents by affixing a bronze snake to a pole. Final preparations for the conquest of Canaan included a census and delineation of the Promised Land. Moses appointed Joshua as his successor. In his last days he ascended Mt. Nebo to deliver his farewell address (largely the book of Deuteronomy). He recounted Israel's recent history and the laws of the covenant, predicting that God will send other prophets like himself. He sang a prophetic song, blessed the tribes, beheld Canaan from afar and died at the age of one hundred and twenty. According to the Bible, Moses was buried by God Himself, which is why till date nobody knows exactly where Moses was buried.

A number of leadership lessons can be gleaned from Moses' story.

- Moses exhibited a zeal and passion for leadership right from early manhood in his genuine compassion for his people. Every leadership role requires a good dose of zeal and passion for change.

- Moses received some leadership training even in his role as a shepherd in Midian. Effective leadership requires training no matter how passionate you are about the role.

- Fear is normal in leadership. What is not normal is when you fail to overcome that fear to act. Moses overcame his initial fears of embarking on his assignment and carried it through.

- Moses' leadership was largely specific: to bring the children of Israel from Egypt to the Promised Land. Effective leadership expresses itself in specificity of the leadership assignment.

- Challenges and disappointments are normal in leadership as exemplified by the myriad of challenges that Moses faced as a leader.

- Moses succeeded largely because of his Obedience and strong relationship with God. Apart from God we are nothing as leaders.

- Moses also displayed firmness and perseverance as a leader.

Having perused Moses' leadership assignment tracks, let us now turn our attention to another leader who created a niche for himself as far as effective leadership is concerned; Alexander III of Macedonia (or Macedon), commonly known as Alexander the Great. Indeed, from a historical point of view Alexander the Great stands out as an exceptional leader. He is considered one of the greatest military geniuses of all times. He was born in 356 BC in Pella, the ancient capital of Macedonia. He was son of Philip II, king of Macedonia, and Olympias, the princess of neighbouring Epirus. Alexander spent his childhood watching his father transform Macedonia into a great military power, winning victory after victory on the battlefields throughout the Balkans. At age twelve he showed his equestrian skill to his father and all who were watching when he tamed Bucephalus, an unruly stallion horse, unable to be ridden and devouring the flesh of all who had tried.

When Alexander was 13, his father hired the Greek philosopher Aristotle to be Alexander's personal tutor. During the next three years Aristotle gave Alexander training in rhetoric and literature and stimulated his interest in science, medicine, and philosophy, all of which became of importance in Alexander's later life. In 340 BC when the king invaded Thrace, he left 16 year old Alexander with the power to rule Macedonia in his absence as Regent, which shows that even at that young age Alexander was recognized as quite capable. But as the Macedonian army advanced deep into Thrace, the Thracian tribe of Maedi bordering north eastern Macedonia rebelled and posed a danger to Macedonia. Alexander assembled an army, led it against the rebels, and with swift action defeated the Maedi, captured their stronghold, and renamed it after himself to Alexandropolis. Two years later in 338 BC, King Philip gave Alexander a commanding post among the senior generals as the Macedonian army invaded Greece. At the battle of Chaeronea the Greeks were defeated and Alexander displayed his bravery by destroying the elite Greek force, the Theban Secret Band. Some ancient historians recorded that the Macedonians won the battle thanks to his bravery.

But not too long after the defeat of the Greeks at Chaeronea, the royal family split apart when the king married Cleopatra, a Macedonian girl of high nobility. At the wedding banquet, Cleopatra's uncle, General Attalus, made a remark about the king fathering a 'legitimate' heir, i.e., one that was of pure Macedonian blood. Alexander threw his cup at the man, blasting him for calling him 'bastard child'. The king stood up, drew his sword, and charged at Alexander, only to trip and fall on his face in his drunken stupor at which Alexander shouted: "Here is the man who was making ready to cross from Europe to Asia, and who cannot even cross from one table to another without losing his balance". He then took his mother and fled Macedonia to Epirus, his mother's country. Although Alexander was allowed to return to Macedonia later, he remained isolated and insecure at the Macedonian court.

In the spring of 336 BC, with the king's invasion of Persia already set in motion, the king was assassinated by a young Macedonian noble called Pausanias. Pausanias was instantly put to death by Alexander's close friends as he attempted to flee the scene, instead of being captured alive and tried before the Macedonian assembly. King Philip

II was succeeded by his son Alexander III. The king's death caused series of rebellions among the conquered nations and the Illyrians, Thracians, and Greeks saw a chance for independence. Alexander acted swiftly. He forced his way into Greece despite the roads leading to the country being blocked by the Thessalians. As soon as he restored Macedonian rule in northern Greece, he marched into Southern Greece. His speed surprised the Greeks and by the end of summer 336 BC they had no other choice but to acknowledge his authority.

Believing that Greece would remain calm, Alexander returned to Macedonia, marched east into Thrace, and campaigned as far as the Danube river. He defeated the Thracians and Tribalians in series of battles and drove the rebels beyond the river. Then he marched back across Macedonia and on his return crushed in a single week the threatening Illyrians, before they could receive additional reinforcements.

Upon rumours of Alexander's death (which was false), a major revolt broke out in Greece that engulfed the whole nation. Enraged, Alexander marched south covering 240 miles in two weeks and appeared before the walls of Thebes with a large

Macedonian army. He let the Greeks know that it was not too late for them to change their minds, but the Thebans, confident in their position called for all the Greeks who wished to set Greece free to join them against the Macedonians. They were not aware that the Athenians and the Peloponnesians, stunned by the speed of the Macedonian king, quickly reconsidered their options and were now awaiting the outcome of the battle before they made their next move.

Alexander's general Perdiccas attacked the gates, broke into the city, and Alexander moved with the rest of the army behind him to prevent the Thebans from cutting him off. The Macedonians stormed the city, killing everyone in sight, women and children included. Six thousand Thebans citizens died and thirty thousand more were sold as slaves. This was to be an example to the rest of Greece and Athens and the other Greek city-states quickly rethought their quest for freedom. Greece remained under Macedonian rule.

Alexander masterminded and led several other battles such as the Battle of Granicus, campaigns in Asia Minor, Battle of Issus, Sieges of Tyre and Gaza, and the Conquest of Egypt. Alexander entered

Egypt in the beginning of 331 BC. The Persian satrap surrendered and the Macedonians were welcomed by the Egyptians as liberators for they (the Egyptians) had despised living under Persian rule for almost two centuries. Here, Alexander ordered that a city be designed and founded in his name at the mouth of River Nile as a trading cum military outpost, the first of many to come. He never lived to see it built but Alexandria, the name of the city, later became a major economic and cultural center in the Mediterranean world not only during the Macedonian rule in Egypt but centuries after.

In the spring of 331 BC Alexander made a pilgrimage to the great temple and oracle of Amon-Ra, the Egyptian god of the sun, whom the Greeks and Macedonians identified with Zeus Ammon. The earlier Egyptian Pharaohs were believed to be sons of Amon-Ra and Alexander as new ruler of Egypt wanted the god to acknowledge him as his son. He decided to make the dangerous trip across the desert to visit the oracle at the temple of the god. According to the legend, on the way he was blessed with abundant rain, and guided across the desert by ravens. At the temple he was welcomed by the priests and spoke to the oracle. The priest told him that he was a son of Zeus Ammon, destined to rule the world, and this must have confirmed in him his belief of divine origin. Alexander remained in Egypt until the middle of 331, and then returned to Tyre before facing Darius, king of Persia.

At Tyre, Alexander received reinforcements from Europe, reorganized his forces, and started for Babylon. He conquered the lands between rivers Tigris and Euphrates and found the Persian army at the plains of Gaugamela, near modern Irbil in Iraq. The Macedonians spotted the lights from the Persian campfires and encouraged Alexander to lead his attack under cover of darkness. But he refused to take advantage of the situation because he wanted to defeat Darius in an equally matched battle so that the Persian king would never again dare to raise an army against him. The two armies met on the battlefield the next morning, October 1, 331 BC. After a series of squabbles, Alexander finally found king Darius dead in his coach, apparently assassinated by Bessus, the satrap of Bactria.

To win the support of the Persian aristocracy Alexander appointed many Persians as provincial governors in his new empire. He adopted the Persian dress for ceremonies, gave orders for

Persians to be enlisted in the army, and encouraged the Macedonians to marry Persian women. But the Macedonians were unhappy with Alexander's orientalization for they were proud of their Macedonian customs, culture, and language. His increasingly Oriental behavior eventually led to conflict with the Macedonian nobles and some Greeks in the train. In 330 BC series of allegations were brought up against some of Alexander's officers concerning a plot to murder him. These allegations sparked a house cleaning exercise which saw the torture and execution of Macedonian nobles and senior officers of the army.

In the spring of 324 BC, after his march with his army into India (in 327 BC), Alexander held a great victory celebration at Susa. He and eighty of his close associates married Persian noblewomen. Little later, at Opis, Alexander proclaimed the discharge of ten thousand Macedonian veterans to be sent home to Macedonia with General Craterus. Craterus' orders were to replace Antipater and Antipater's to bring new reinforcements in Asia. But the army mutinied hearing this. Enraged, Alexander pointed the main ringleaders to his bodyguards to be punished and then gave his famous speech where he reminded

15

the Macedonians that without him and his father, late king Philip, they would have still been living in fear of the nations surrounding Macedonia, instead of ruling the world. After this the Macedonians were reconciled with their king, and ten thousand of them set out for Europe, leaving their children of Asian women with Alexander. In the same time thirty thousand Persian youth already trained in Macedonian manner were recruited in the army. Alexander prayed for unity between Macedonians and Persians and by breeding a new army of mixed blood he hoped to create a core of a new royal army which would be attached only to him.

But shortly before the beginning of the planned Arabian campaign, he contracted a high fever after attending a private party at his friend's Medius of Larisa. As soon as he drank from the cup he "shrieked aloud as if smitten by a violent blow". The fever became stronger with each following day to the point that he was unable to move and speak. The Macedonians were allowed to file past their leader for the last time before he finally succumbed to the illness on June 7, 323 BC. Alexander the Great, the Macedonian king and the great conqueror of Persian Empire, died at the age of thirty-three.

Like Moses, Alexander the Great's leadership potential was also obvious from an early age. His leadership assignment was also clear cut: to make Macedonia the ruler of the world. He exhibited bravery, perseverance, strategic thinking and passion for success.

The above two case studies and others across the globe point to the critical role of leadership in ensuring effective growth and development of families, associations, communities, societies and nations. In line with this importance, several books have been written on the topic of leadership. This book is an addition to the growing number of books and knowledge on the topic. But more importantly, it presents the subject of leadership in a very simplified form thereby making it easily comprehensible and useful to all. More so when leadership is required at various levels of society, right from the family to the national level, including formal and informal groups, institutions, associations and organizations.

The thoughts behind this book were developed through the author's: formal education which included study of some aspects of leadership; informal reading of various books on leadership; and leadership experiences at various levels.

# CHAPTER TWO

## WHAT IS LEADERSHIP ALL ABOUT?

### 2:1    INTRODUCTION

Leadership is one of the oldest biblical and social institutions in the history of mankind. Right from the Garden of Eden God ordained Adam as a leader over Eve giving him specific roles and functions to perform. As man segregated into groups in the form of families, clans, communities, societies, associations, organizations, and nations, the concept of leadership assumed a more important role in terms of the provision of guidance, support, and inspiration to enable a group address its needs, aspirations, problems and/or challenges for growth and survival. Examples of Moses, Joshua, David, etc. in the Bible testify to this.

Proving guidance, support, and inspiration to a group requires various forms of resources such as time, money, property, natural resources, attitude, skills, knowledge etc. Leadership can therefore be appropriately defined as the utilization of resources by a person(s) to undertake activities that address the needs, aspirations, problems and/or challenges of the group to ensure growth and survival as well as the achievement of the group's vision and goals. The large majority who are led are normally referred to as followers.

Group, the generic term for a collection of people who interact on the basis of shared expectations of each others' behaviour and have common goals, is the main focus of every leader's actions. We noted earlier on that groups come in the form of family, association, organization, community, nation etc. Thus in discussing leadership, it is important and critical for us to gain some insight into the basic nature of groups, be it family, association, organization or community.

## 2:2   NATURE OF GROUPS

In general, groups have features that provide meaning to their existence and invariably influence their activities and performance. These features include mission, philosophy, objectives and goals, structure, process, resources, and culture. The specific nature of the features differs from one group to the other.

Thus, by plan or default, groups are established with a mission, philosophy, objectives, and goals. Groups also operate with certain basic resources including human, materials and technology; they adopt basic strategies, methods and skills for their work and develop a unique culture over time. It is therefore necessary for leaders to know and understand these features.

## 2:2:1   Mission

The mission of a group establishes the parameters within which it is to function. The mission of a group is usually a statement about the origin, legal basis, clientele, reasons for existence, and types of programmes to be generated. A good understanding of the mission of the group will guide the leader's efforts in planning. The mission of a group also states the task that the group was formed to undertake or achieve. Sometimes the mission statement could even give a clue about the geographical coverage of the group. All activities of the group, including the planning of programmes, are therefore guided by this basic mission. In this regard, it is important for leaders to always have the mission of their group in mind to guide their work.

The mission of a group clearly indicates the group's mandate, eliminating any ambiguity in what the group is expected to do. It therefore serves as an important reminder to the leader, group members and all stakeholders. The mission enables the group to concentrate their efforts and attention on activities to be undertaken, ensuring unity of purpose and company cohesion. It also provides an identity to the members of the group and projects the image of the group. A good understanding of the mission of the group is an important guide to the activities of the group at all levels.

There is no hard and fast rule about the content of a mission statement. The important thing is for the statement to give a very clear indication of what the group stands for. It is usually stated in general terms but at the same time specific enough to know what the group is all about. A mission statement may, generally, be defined as a concise, inspirational statement of purpose, including fundamental values and beliefs that reflect the unique nature of a group – it is built or formulated from an understanding of a group's mandate, values and strengths.

## 2:2:2   Philosophy

Beliefs and values go a long way to influence people's choices and actions. A person is likely to work very hard if he believes that hard work conquers all. In the same way a person who values life is likely to treat others and himself with dignity. Beliefs and values of a person together make up an individual's philosophy. Like individuals, groups also have philosophies. The philosophy of a group embodies its beliefs and values framework or system. These beliefs and values of the group drive its choices and actions and to a large extent distinguish it from other groups. Some of the beliefs and values of groups include: honesty; integrity; hard work; transparency; accountability; life after death; etc.

## 2:2:3   Objectives and Goals

Objectives and goals refer to targets we set for ourselves; in relation to goals, objectives are short term targets considered as intermediate steps to achieving goals (long-term targets). Goals could be considered as a destination, with objectives as the milestones along the way. Groups, such as associations and corporate organisations are established with objectives and goals which emanate from their mission. Beyond the objectives and goals that are set for groups during the foundation stage, programmes planned for the group also come with objectives and goals that are expected to have their origin in the contemporary needs of members of the group and constitute the framework within which all decisions and actions about the group's activities must be linked.

## 2:2:4   Group Structure

To undertake their activities effectively and efficiently, groups operate with a structure.   A group's structure may be defined simply as the various positions and roles in a group and how those positions and roles relate to each other.  There are two main types of group structure, namely bureaucracy and democracy.  It is important to note that there are other types of organisational structure such as power culture and matrix.

Bureaucracy is a group structure with the following features:

- The group contains a clear-cut division of labour – every member is responsible for particular tasks.  For instance, the task of the Managing Director of an organisation run along bureaucratic lines is clearly different from that of the Human Resource Manager of the same organisation.

- Authority is organised in a hierarchy – everyone, except the leader, reports to someone whose directive are to be obeyed. In other words one level of activity is subject to control by the next higher level.
- The activities of all members of the group are governed by a set of formally established rules and regulations. These rules and regulations are expected to be obeyed to the letter by all members of the organisation.
- Members carry out their group responsibilities impartially and without the exercise of favouritism or bias towards others.
- Recognition, rewards and status in the group are based upon merit.
- There is separation of officials from the ownership of the group. A typical example is the distinction between shareholders of an organisation and the board of directors. The shareholders own the organisation and the board of directors and managers are involved in the day-to-day operations of the organisation.
- Organisational positions exist in their own rights and the job holders have no right to a particular position.

Bureaucracy exists to a greater or lesser extent in practically every business and public enterprise. Most work settings are therefore organised along bureaucratic principles. The organisational chart of a bureaucratic organisational structure shows the different hierarchical levels and the different functional areas that derive from division of labour.

Although bureaucracy has been acclaimed as the most efficient means of organising for the achievement of group goals and objectives, there are several weaknesses in the bureaucratic model

- Rules, originally designed to serve group efficiency have a tendency to become all important in their own right. A very simple example is where a staff, in obedience to the organisation's rules, would rather go through laid down procedures to seek official approval to speak to a client he chanced on in town rather than taking advantage of the situation to discuss a business deal. In the same vein it kills initiative since office holders are forced to obey existing procedures.
- Relationships between office holders or roles are based on the rights and duties of each role, i.e. they are depersonalised.

This leads to rigid behaviour. This occurs because all officials are careful to stick to the rules and regulations governing their positions to the detriment of their personal relationship with other office holders.

- For many workers some consequences of bureaucratic control include dissatisfaction and alienation.

Whereas bureaucracy literally involves control of people, democracy involves control by people. Under bureaucracy most people have little or no power to shape the policies that affect them; but in a democracy people are empowered to participate in shaping those policies. Democratic organisational models reflect political values that view personal empowerment and involvement as fundamental goal. There is the need to differentiate between direct democracy and representative democracy. In direct democracy all members participate in decision-making. In representative democracy people elect others to make decisions for them. Direct democracy is one means by which all members can express their needs and work with others in getting those needs met.

Key features of groups run on democratic principles are:

- Power is shared within the membership as a whole and decision-making involves discussions, negotiation and consensus.
- Rules are minimal, members are assumed to be capable of using discretion and common sense in conducting their activities.
- There is a sense of community. People do not limit their interaction to the work tasks at hand but feel free to develop close relationship with one another.
- The division of labour is minimal. Members share their knowledge and take turns rotating jobs when possible.
- Just as there is no hierarchy of authority, rewards are shared equally or nearly so.

Democratic organisations also face some bottlenecks such as:

- Democratic decision making can be time consuming.
- Differences among group members can at times be very intense and disturbing.
- Majority rule under democratic decision-making is not a protection against poor decisions.

These two types of structures feed into the concept of leadership style which is mentioned later in the book.

### 2:2:5   Group Processes

Groups grow and develop by performing various activities. These activities are undertaken by leaders and members alike. In undertaking these activities various procedures and measures are followed all of which are geared towards achieving the goals and objectives of the group. These procedures and measures are generally referred to as group processes. Some of these group processes are usually captured in the constitution of the group. For instance the constitution spells out how a person is admitted into the group, the sanctions for misbehaviour, appointment or election of leaders, payment of financial commitments etc.

### 2:2:6   Resources

Resource, in this context refers to the means available to achieve an end or fulfil a function. Resource could be in the form of human (personnel), equipment, material, teaching aids, technology, vehicles and sources of funding, all of which are needed for the smooth operation of an organisation.

### 2:2:7   Organisational Culture

As an organisation grows, it develops a unique way of doing things that together could be described as its culture.  Organisational culture refers to the material (code of dressing, vehicle, building etc.) and non-material aspects (norms, values, knowledge, attitude to work etc.) of the lifestyle shared and transmitted among the members of an organization. It comes in the form of the way members dress, their level of discipline, extent of communication among members, attitude to clients of the organisation and so on.

Thus, in providing guidance, support and inspiration to a group, a leader must be knowledgeable about the above features of his group in order to provide a leadership that is in sync with the nature of the group. That is what leadership is all about.

### 2:3   SOME FACTS ABOUT LEADERSHIP

In discussing leadership it is important to explore some facts about it:

- As noted above, leadership does not occur only at the national level of a country.  And for emphasis, let me stress that leadership is not the preserve of the President of a country.

Per the definition outlined above, leadership occurs everywhere you find a collection of people who interact or act together on the basis of shared expectations of each other's behaviour and have common interests, goals, objectives or vision, what we generally refer to as a group. So leadership occurs in the classroom in the position and role of a class captain; in a school as school prefect; in the family as parents, father or mother; in an organization as Chief Executive Officer; in an association as Chairman, Convenor or President; in a village or town as Chief; in a Church as Pope, Archbishop, Bishop, General Overseer or Pastor; in a government ministry as Minister; etc. In practice, all those who assist persons who occupy the above leadership positions are also considered as part of leadership.

• It needs to be stressed that leadership is the most crucial element in all growth and developmental agenda of groups. Even though followers also have their role to play in the growth and development of the group, the bulk of the responsibility lies at the doorstep of leadership. The blame game that ensues between leaders and followers when groups fail, in my view, is neither here nor there. It is the responsibility of every leader to influence his/her followers to succeed. Anything short of that is a failure on the part of the leader.

• A cursory view of various leadership positions and the persons that occupy those positions point to the fact that, with the exception of royal positions, leadership is not for a select few. In other words, every person has the potential to lead. Also related to this point is the reality that several people occupy leadership positions without knowing the rudiments of leadership, hence fail to perform their leadership roles effectively.

• Closely related to the point above is my personal conviction that leadership can be learned and applied; and that is my position on the age-old argument about whether leaders are born or made. The point is that leadership excels on the wings of certain human traits, innate and/or acquired. A person who has a good dose of innate traits that support leadership is likely to excel at his/her leadership role. However, a person who has little innate leadership traits can also acquire leadership traits to excel in a leadership position.

- A critical study of various leaders suggests that leadership comes in various shapes and forms generally referred to as Leadership Style. Leadership Style is therefore defined as the manner and approach of providing direction, inspiration and guidance for a group to achieve its objectives. Three main styles of leadership can be identified – authoritarian, participative, and delegation. In the authoritarian style, the leader tells his subordinates what he wants done and how he wants it done, without getting their advice. In the participative style of leadership, the leader includes one or more of his subordinates in the decision-making process (determining what to do and how to do it). However, the leader maintains the final decision-making authority. In the delegation style of leadership, the leader allows the subordinates to make the decisions. However, the leader is still responsible for the decisions that are made. Although most leaders use all three styles, one of them becomes the dominant one. Factors that influence the style to be used, include a number of things such as; amount of time available, basis of relationship between the leader and subordinates (i.e. trust or disrespect), who has the necessary information (you, your employees or both), type of task to be undertaken (structured, or unstructured; complicated or simple), and laws or established procedures. *Leadership skill*, then, refers to the ability of a manager to blend the three main leadership styles (i.e. authoritarian, participative, and delegation) appropriately in every given situation.

- God uses leaders to meet needs of people & establish His will on earth (e.g. Joseph, Moses, Gideon, etc).

As I end this chapter, I need to stress the vast gulf between "leadership" and "effective leadership". Leadership points to the incidental performance of various roles and activities by a person or persons occupying leadership positions in a group that may or may not impact positively on the group. Effective leadership, on the other hand, points to the deliberate performance of roles and activities that result in addressing the aspirations, needs, challenges and problems of a group. So I guess one could say "everybody can be a leader but not everybody can be an effective leader". The focus of this book is on *effective leadership* where a person or persons occupying leadership positions in a group deliberately position themselves to undertake the functions expected of them as enabled by time tested traits and qualities.

# CHAPTER THREE

## BASIC LEADERSHIP FUNCTIONS

### 3:1 INTRODUCTION

As we noted in the first two chapters, leadership involves the performance of several and various activities to inspire, support, guide and help groups (family, community, association, organization, nation etc) to achieve their objectives and goals. To put these activities in proper perspective, I have categorized them into four (4) functions namely:

- ✓ Planning.
- ✓ Implementation of planned and contingent activities.
- ✓ Monitoring.
- ✓ Evaluation.

Thus all activities performed by leaders can be placed firmly under one of the four basic functions listed above. It is important to note that leaders work closely with assistants, deputies and other staff, so it is probably prudent to state that leaders spearhead the above functions. We shall study each of these functions into details in this chapter.

## 3:2   PLANNING AS A LEADER'S FUNCTION

Planning is a very basic function of leadership and any leader who ignores planning does so at his peril. One of the triumph cards of a good leader is his ability to plan effectively for his group. There are various definitions of planning, but generally, planning involves making wise or well thought-out decisions for the future based on an understanding of the present situation and other available or relevant information; that is, an attempt to make choices or decisions for the future in the present or now. In other words, it involves deciding in advance what to do, how to do it, when to do it, and who to do it. It could also be considered as an organised intelligent attempt to select the best available alternatives to achieve specific goals. As implied above, planning is basically an attempt to be proactive rather than reactive and it is based on the presumption that if we know where we are now, and where we ought to go, we can better judge what to do and how to do it.

It must be emphasised that planning as a concept is based on a number of assumptions that gives meaning and purpose to the process. Raudabaugh and Leagans outlined eleven of such assumptions; these are presented in an abridged form as follows:

- Human growth and development is an endless process which naturally outlives successive leaders. Thus leaders succeed each other to continue the developmental process of a growth. One leader may initiate an idea for another leader who succeeds him to continue or implement it. Leaders need to bear this in mind.

- The means and ways for solving most human problems are available and can be found.

- It is possible to select, organise, and administer certain resources of knowledge, technology, personnel, physical environment and teaching/learning methods to help people achieve a more desirable quality of life.

- The knowledge and skills of professionals can be meshed with the knowledge and skills of the members of a group to find optimum solutions to the group's problems.

- Change is sometimes desirable and necessary but change for the sake of change is not always desirable. Groups can be helped to make wise choices in adopting new behaviour or in preserving old and cherished ones.

- The basis for decisions for change should not be taken lightly, but rather should be considered carefully.

- People will usually accept new modes of thinking and doing things in favour of present ones if the new ones are perceived as offering certain advantages and having sufficient aesthetic appeal.

Being assumptions, the above points are accepted as 'true' as far as planning by leaders is considered and therefore provides a premise for the planning process.

### 3:2:1   Steps in Planning

Effective planning involves undertaking six (6) clearly defined but interrelated steps that result in the development of a blueprint of activities to be undertaken to ensure the growth and development of the group.  The six (6) steps are:

#### 3:2:1:1 *Situation Analysis*

Situation Analysis, as the name implies, involves a detailed analysis of a group by a leader to gain a comprehensive understanding of the group. Specifically, it involves the collection of data about a group, the analysis of the data, and the use of the information obtained to guide other planning activities.  Data collected during this exercise also includes data that may be external to the group but considered relevant to the survival of the group.

In collecting the data, the leader must determine what specific data to collect, why it is necessary to collect it, where to collect it, who to collect it from, and how to collect it. Information obtained from situation analysis must be well documented for immediate use and for future reference. As noted above, it serves as a guide to other planning activities as well as implementation, monitoring and evaluation.

In conducting a situation analysis, the leader of say a Hotels Association may collect data such as: number of registered members of the association, star ratings of members' hotels, directors and/or general managers of member hotels, location of member hotels in the association's geographical jurisdiction, number of rooms of each hotel and other facilities in the hotel, state policies and laws that govern the hotel industry, nature of other hotel associations in the geographical area if any, regulatory bodies of the hotel industry, public perception of the hotel industry etc. On the other hand, in undertaking situation analysis, the leader of a church congregation is likely to gather information such as: size of the congregation in terms of registered members and casual visitors, gender distribution of members, business occupation of members, residential location of members, spiritual and physical needs of members, the state laws and policies that govern religious bodies etc. The Chief Executive Officer of a bank may also gather information on: population size of clients; gender distribution of the clients; occupation of the clients; various transactions undertaken by clients at the bank: economic environment of the bank; client distribution across the various branches of the bank etc.

### 3:2:1:2 *Problem Analysis*

After obtaining comprehensive information and understanding of a group, a leader needs to go deeper by analyzing all problems or challenges facing the group that was identified during the situation analysis. Specifically, Problem Analysis involves determining the possible causes of a problem, determining the alternative solutions to the problem and deciding on the best solution as guided by existing opportunities, threats and gaps in the group. One of the time tested tools for undertaking problem analysis is the Problem Tree. A Problem tree is simply a diagram that shows the relationship between a core or focal problem and the various factors that may have contributed to creating it (problem). The relationship between contributing factors is indicated by arrows.

A good problem analysis provides a sound foundation based on which relevant and focused programme objectives are formulated. Where necessary, a leader needs to solicit the assistance of experts to enable him undertake an effective analysis of the group's problems.

### 3:2:1:3 Setting Targets

Once a leader receives an in-depth understanding of the problems confronting his group through problem analysis, he is in a strategic position to set targets that serve as a focus for achievement. Setting targets involves deciding on the goals and/ or objectives to be achieved based on the group's challenges and aspirations. As indicated in an earlier chapter, objectives are short term targets that are considered as intermediate steps to achieving goals (long term targets). Objectives and goals serve as the main focus that drives a group into action. They also provide the basis for monitoring and evaluation and therefore must be well formulated to serve their purpose.

A good goal/objective is therefore expected to be specific, measurable, achievable; realistic, and time bound (SMART). An objective is described as: 'Specific' if it defines exactly what is to be achieved; 'Measureable' if it contains elements that can be measured; 'Achievable' if the time available is adequate for undertaking the activities; 'Realistic' if resources can be accessed to undertake the activities; and 'Time-Bound' if the objective contains a time element that indicates how long it would take to achieve it.

### 3:2:1:4 Development of an action plan

Goals and Objectives achieve nothing by themselves until they are translated into a set of activities to be undertaken by the leader and his group members. The set of activities so generated, plus when to do it, how to do it, who to do it, resources needed, and expected results culminate in what is generally known as an Action Plan.

The Action Plan takes center stage during implementation where the leader and his group members undertake activities in the Action Plan to ensure the achievement of the set Goals and Objectives. The logic is that the activities are developed from the Goals and Objectives, hence the implementation of those activities are expected to achieve the Goals and Objectives. For example, a leader identifies low morale among staff as the cause of poor services to clients. Further analysis of the situation points to low salary, bad policies and poor welfare benefits. Based on these findings, the leader needs to set targets to address the problems and those targets would lead to undertaking activities such as increasing salary to a point over a specific period, changing all policies perceived to be bad and reviewing welfare policies that are perceived as poor by workers. Once these activities are carried out, they are expected to result in achievement of the set targets because they were derived from them.

### 3:2:1:5 Budgeting

Even though budgeting may be considered as part of Action Plan development, it is separated here for emphasis. Budgeting is crucial in every planning process because all activities to be implemented have implications for resource use and it is important to know how much of those resources shall be needed to ensure effective implementation. Budgeting basically involves determining the cost to be incurred in the implementation of the action plan, as well as the expected revenue.

### 3:2:1:6 Documentation

Generally, documentation of the planning process is expected to commence right at the beginning of the process. In other words, every decision that is made or information that is gathered during the first five (5) stages of planning must be articulately documented as a guide for subsequent activities. At the end of the planning process, it is important to assemble all these information into a document known as the Plan or Program. The outline of the document can be as follows:

i.      Title of the Document
ii.     Date
iii.    Background information of the Group
iv.     Problems Identified
v.      Objectives and Goals for the Group
vi.     Action Plan
vii.    Budget

The activities enumerated in the six (6) steps of planning could go on concurrently for as many projects or programmes that a leader is involved in. This implies that a leader could be involved in the situation analysis stage of planning for a particular programme at the same time that he is also involved in the development of an action plan for another programme. The important thing is for the leader to diligently follow the six planning steps for each endeavour that he undertakes for his group. With experience in planning on his side, a leader may require less time and effort to go through the six (6) steps of planning. But that will also depend on the nature of the endeavour. Obviously some endeavours would require more time and effort to going through the planning process irrespective of the leader's experience.

### 3:2:2 Approaches to Planning

In undertaking the above six (6) planning steps, a leader has the option to choose one of two major approaches: the Top-down approach or the Bottom-up approach. The two approaches can be distinguished based on the extent to which the leader (and presumably his executive team) and the followers are involved in decision-making related to stages in the planning process.

### 3:2:2:1 *Top-down Approach*

In a typical Top-Down Approach, also referred to as the Directive Approach, the leader and his executive team go through the six planning steps to develop a programme and present it to the group for approval and implementation. In other words, most of the decisions in the planning process are taken by the leader and his executive team hence group members play a passive role in the process. Thus, for group members for whom all this is done, participation in the preliminary phase of the project may at best consist of meetings where they are informed about the project's objectives and activities

### 3:2:2:2 *Bottom-up Approach*

In the Bottom-Up approach, also referred to as participatory approach, the leader empowers the people to go through the six planning steps to develop a programme which is presented to the leader and his executive team for approval and implementation. There are various permutations of the two major approaches where the leader and his executive team engage the group members in various stages of the planning process.

Even though the Bottom-Up approach has been touted as the preferred choice in the development of programmes that are likely to be accepted by the generality of a group, the Top-down approach also has its advantages particularly in situations where time is of essence.

### 3:2:3 Uncertainties in Planning

The time lag between planning and implementation, no matter how short it may be, subjects planning to various uncertainties. Uncertainty refers to situations where it is not possible to attach probabilities to the occurrence of events that are likely to affect the outcome of a decision making process. The importance attached to uncertainty in planning is related to the potential effect of various events that may occur between the time when planning is undertaken and the time when the plan or programme is actually implemented. Uncertainties may occur in the form of natural disasters (flooding, earthquake), health challenges (disease outbreak etc); industrial action (strikes); market fluctuations (changes in prices of goods and services); social issues (conflicts) and state actions (changes in policies). If such changes are expected and taken care of during planning then they cease to be uncertainties.

The effects of the above uncertainties on planning may vary from one situation to the other; some may have insignificant effect whilst others may result in the disruption of planned activities, hence bringing all the efforts in planning to naught. Much as leaders (planners) cannot stop such uncertainties from occurring, they can develop some capacity and capability to address them when they occur, hence they should not be overlooked.

### 3:2:4   Planning Levels

Depending on the size and complexity of a group, a leader may undertake planning at various levels. Planning level refers to a geographical or administrative boundary relevant to a particular planning process. For instance, in the Ghana Hotels Association where I served as the Chairman of the Greater Accra Regional Branch (at the time of writing this book), I spearheaded planning for that geographical or administrative area. Other regional chairpersons also spearheaded planning for their respective areas. Our National President, presiding over all the eleven administrative areas of the association also spearheaded planning for the entire eleven administrative areas. The important thing here is for the leader to know his geographical or administrative boundary and undertake his planning accordingly.

### 3:2:5   Span of Planning

Time is a very important element in planning. It finds expression in the setting of objectives and goals where planners state the timeframe within which a target is expected to be met or achieved. Depending on the time required for the achievement of targets, planning could be termed as short term, medium term or long term. Short term planning spans up to about five years; medium term planning is between 5 and 10 years; and long term planning is 10 years and beyond. These timeline definitions may differ from one project to another or from one group to another. Leaders must always be cognizant of the duration of their plans to enable them direct their efforts appropriately.

### 3:2:6   A tip on Planning

So far we have looked at the technical aspect of planning where a leader follows some prescribed steps to develop a programme for his group. Beyond the technical aspect of planning, it is important for a leader to appreciate the several other planning-related roles that he has to play to make the planning process effective and acceptable to group members. Those roles fall under three main categories, namely interpersonal role, informational role, and decisional role.

The interpersonal role of a leader requires him to act as a link between his group and other groups or stakeholders and generally forge a healthy working relationship among group members and all relevant stakeholders. In planning, a leader performs this role to ensure a healthy working relationship among all persons involved in the planning process. A leader who performs this role effectively and efficiently is able to get the best out of participants in the planning process.

The informational role of a leader generally involves the giving and receiving of information. Information is vital to the planning of a programme. A leader must gather all information relevant to the planning of a programme and make the information available to all persons involved in the planning process. An effective leader knows what information to keep and which ones to distribute.

The decisional role of a leader during planning requires him to use information received plus his own initiative to make decisions that enhance the planning process. Several decisions are made during the planning process and a leader must be very skilful in decision making to make the right decisions. Poor or bad decisions can be very costly and leaders must learn to get it right.

## 3:3    IMPLEMENTATION AS A LEADER'S FUNCTION

The second basic function of a leader is Implementation. After utilizing scarce resources to plan a programme, the next thing that an effective leader does is to spearhead the implementation of the planned programme. Simply put, implementation involves carrying out activities specified in the action plan of the programme as well as other contingent activities needed to achieve the set goals/objectives. More specifically, Implementation involves the transformation of means (equipment, money, human resource, organisation, and management skills) and activities into output. This usually involves mobilization, organisation and facilitation of resources, members of the group, and other relevant stakeholders.

As implied above, the action plan serves as the main guide during the implementation of the programme by specifying what is to be done, where it is to be done, when it is to be done, how it is to be done, who is to do it, and the resources needed. The success of a programme depends, to a large extent, on how well it is implemented and how conducive the environment (natural, physical, social, economic, policy etc) is. In other words, if the environment 'behaves' as anticipated during planning and the leader, his executive team, his group members, and other stakeholders undertake the various activities in the action plan competently, then there is a high probability for achievement of programme objectives.

Obviously the leader does not implement the activities alone; he does it with the support and involvement of his executive team, members of the group and relevant stakeholders. Thus technically, the leader spearheads implementation. At this stage, a leader's power of influence needs to be activated to enable him get his executive team, members of the group, and indeed all stakeholders to participate in all activities in the action plan.

In spearheading the implementation of planned programmes, leaders also play the interpersonal, informational, and decisional roles similar to what they do during planning i.e. serving as a link between various segments of the group, and between the group and external stakeholders relevant to the implementation of the programme; capturing all information relevant to the implementation and making same available to all; and making decisions that enhance the implementation of the programme.

It is important to note that there is no single best way to manage the implementation of a programme. The way chosen will depend on the mission, goals and objectives of the organisation, the objectives and goals of the programme as well as the group members and the situation in which the group operates. The important thing is for a leader to understand the unique features of his group (which is different from other groups) and the programme and perform his leadership roles in accordance with the task and situations under which the group operates.

It is also important to note that several things may occur to disrupt the implementation of a well planned programme. Some disruptions can be contained or resolved for the programme to continue but others might be of such magnitude as to result in the abrupt end or termination of the programme. Disruptions may include natural disasters, emergence of factions opposed to the programme, conflicts, war, illnesses that may affect key members and/or stakeholders, loss of interest by members, and changes in government policies.

If a leader is to succeed he has no choice but to implement planned and contingent activities and the only way he can do that is to overcome all obstacles that come his way. This calls for perseverance, patience, commitment and hard work.

## 3:4 MONITORING AS A LEADER'S FUNCTION

Monitoring is a tool for enhancing a leader's effectiveness. It is undertaken during implementation of a programme. Basically, monitoring is the continuous process of checking whether a planned programme is being implemented well and/or according to plan.

The theoretical basis for monitoring can be better explained and appreciated using the action plan. As I noted earlier on, the action plan is the outline of activities which when undertaken (in a conducive environment) is expected to achieve the programme's objectives. A leader has two options as far as carrying out the activities in the action plan is concerned: The first option is to continuously carry out all activities in the action plan, without looking back. The second option is to 'pause' occasionally (or frequently) during implementation to find out if he is on track. The disadvantage with the first option is that significant implementation problems may be overlooked and that can go a long way to negatively affect the outcome or achievement of programme objectives.

The second option, that is pausing occasionally or frequently to find out if execution of activities is on the right track, forms the basis of monitoring. This allows the leader to make adjustments, if necessary, in subsequent execution of activities. Thus by assessing actual progress in implementation against planned progress a leader is able to take some corrective measures, if need be, to ensure the achievement of programme objectives. In other words, monitoring can be considered as a dual task of finding out if the 'right thing' is being done and consequently, ensuring that the 'right thing' is done. In the same vein, we can infer that monitoring enables a leader to make necessary adjustments during implementation of the programme. However, it also serves as a safeguard against unwarranted, unjustified or unauthorised deviation from activities specified in the action plan.

Monitoring is usually undertaken at predetermined phases of the implementation process as a leader deems fit or necessary and involves finding out (among others):

- The activities carried out.
- The methods used to carry out the activities and their appropriateness.
- People or persons reached by the activities, their level of involvement as well as the perception of the usefulness of the activities.
- Resources used, their appropriateness, and adequacy.
- Output of the activities carried.
- Problems encountered, if any.

The above information may be obtained from sources such as reports of officials assigned to those activities and stakeholders. Data collection instruments such as documentary analysis, interviews (questionnaire and checklist), and observations could be used to gather the data. The essence of collecting the above information is to detect short falls in implementation (if any) to allow for remedial action. It is therefore important for the leader to use monitoring reports for such purpose. A monitoring report that is shelved and kept away is tantamount to causing financial loss. Monitoring reports, in addition to its use for improving an ongoing programme, can also serve as an important guide to the planning and implementation of other programmes.

To end this section, I reproduce ten principles of monitoring suggested by Misra.

- Monitoring must be simple. A complex or complicated monitoring system is self-defeating. The basic task of monitoring is to simplify the field-level complexity, sifting the more important concerns from the less important.
- Monitoring must be timely. Timeliness is of the essence in monitoring. A leader requires input from the monitoring system so that timely action may be taken. Also, timeliness is closely related to the credibility of monitoring itself.
- Monitoring must be relevant. It must concern itself only with parameters which are relevant to programme objectives. This also ensures that monitoring does not generate information that is not used or is not usable by the leader.
- Information provided through monitoring should be dependable. A leader will rely on monitoring findings only if the information is believed to be reasonably accurate.
- Monitoring must be flexible. It is iterative

in nature. It also gets routinized with the passage of time. These two features should not, however, lead to rigidity.

- Monitoring should be action oriented. Monitoring often leads to action. Consequently, it should follow pragmatic approaches, keeping the needs of the group in mind all the time. Generating information for which there is no intended use should be assiduously avoided.

- Monitoring must be cost-effective. Monitoring efforts cost money and time. It is therefore essential to make it cost-effective. While principles of simplicity, time-lines, relevance, and accuracy will lead to cost-effectiveness, computerization also can help to make monitoring more cost-effective by reducing staff hours in data processing.

- Monitoring efforts should be leader-oriented. Monitoring units should keep in mind the requirements of a leader when designing and operating a monitoring system. Yet at the same time, monitoring must take into account the fact that those who provide information to the system also must benefit or the quality of the information provided will decline.

- Monitoring units represent specialised undertakings. Monitoring is not merely concerned with the collection and analysis of data, but with diagnosing problems and suggesting alternative practical solutions.

From the foregoing discussion, it is obvious that a leader who values success needs to undertake monitoring of all programmes that he implements. It is also obvious that a leader only spearheads monitoring of programmes and does not necessarily undertake it himself. But he needs to make the effort deployed in monitoring worthwhile by abiding by the principles outlined above.

The use of experts by a leader for monitoring is recommended on the basis of objectivity. This is to suggest that monitoring is likely to be more objective if it is undertaken by experts external to the organization. But a leader could establish a monitoring unit within his setup who can also be objective in the exercise because they are usually semiautonomous.

## 3:5 EVALUATION AS A LEADER'S FUNCTION

Evaluation is the formation of judgment about an item, an event, and indeed anything. It is basically a decision-making process – the process of deciding the value or worth of something. In other words, the process which one goes through to decide or judge the value or worth of something is known as evaluation. A synonym of evaluation is assessment. Evaluation forms an important aspect of our lives. We continuously judge the taste of the food we eat, the wholesomeness of the water we drink; the satisfaction from jobs we do; the attitude of the people we interact with; the importance of the programmes we listen to on the radio or watch on television, and so on. These personal evaluations have become so intrinsically linked with our lives that we seldom take note of them. Furthermore, such evaluations occur so quickly, that they easily pass unnoticed.

Despite our apparent oblivion of our evaluative instincts, the act of evaluation is important in several ways:

    i.    It helps in making the right choices

    ii.    It helps in enhancing our understanding of issues and events

iii.   It helps in shaping our future thoughts and direction

Four main elements can be identified in most, if not all evaluation processes. The elements are: the item to be evaluated; criteria for evaluation; evidence; and judgement.

Evaluation, as mentioned earlier on, is the process of judging or deciding whether something is worthy or has value. Hence evaluation efforts are directed at something, such as an event, an object, a statement etc. That event, object, statement etc. is the 'item to be evaluated'. Criteria refers to our image, idea or understanding of what is good, desirable, suitable or important, and serves as a standard against which we judge situations, events or things. We need to note that such image, idea, or understanding differs from one person to the other, from one society to the other and from one tribe to the other due to differences in scope of knowledge, intelligence, experience, expectation and aspirations. Consciously or unconsciously, we all have some image of what we believe is worthy or desirable and thus are very quick to judge events, situation or things against them. Our image, expectations, and standards of situation, events, or things are usually different from the realities on the ground. That reality is what we refer to as evidence. In other words, evidence, as an element in evaluation, is the fact or reality about that which we are evaluating. Evidence may be subject to peoples' experiences, norms, beliefs, and so on, but represents the 'truth' about that which we are evaluating. Judgement is our decision on the worth or value of that which we are evaluating based on comparing the evidence to the criteria that we have. Depending on our purpose of evaluation and the level of matching between the criteria and the evidence, appropriate decisions are taken.

Thus in evaluation, we first decide on an item, event or thing to evaluate; decide on the criteria; look out for evidence; and then form judgement based on comparing the criteria to the evidence. In our daily evaluation of events, situations or things, we go through these four elements so quickly that we never take cognisance of their role in our judgments or decisions with regards to the worth or value of something.

The basic elements of evaluation as outlined above can be used systematically by a leader to evaluate his programmes. Thus from a leader's perspective, evaluation may be defined as *the formation of judgment about a programme or activity through comparing evidence (what is) with criteria (what should be) and the appropriate utilization of such judgments in the improvement of a programme or activity.* By this definition, evaluation can be undertaken at the three main stages of a programme: during planning, during implementation, and at post-implementation.

Evaluation at the planning stage is generally referred to as *programme appraisal*. Essentially, it is an evaluation of a draft programme to determine whether it is implementation worthy.

Evaluation during implementation of a programme, also referred to as *ongoing evaluation,* is basically concerned with finding out the extent to which a programme is achieving its objectives. Thus it is the *assessment of the worth or value of activities that have been undertaken up to a specified point in the implementation of a programme.* Thus the item being evaluated is the activity or combination of activities that have been undertaken up to a particular point or stage in the implementation of a programme.

The criteria used for ongoing evaluation is developed based on the objectives from which the activities being evaluated were derived. You may recall from earlier discussions that the activities in an action plan of a programme are derived from the objectives of the programme. Thus for each activity in an action plan we also indicate expected changes as a result of undertaking that activity. That expected change is actually a restatement of the sub-objective from which the activity was derived. So that sub-objective (or expected result) is what we expect to achieve when we undertake the activity and therefore serves as the criteria when assessing the worth or value of the activity; it is the standard against which we shall judge the activity.

The evidence in ongoing evaluation is the actual changes that occur as a result of the activities that were undertake. In other words the actual changes, in relation to the activities that were undertaken, at a particular point during implementation represent the reality and serves as the evidence for ongoing evaluation. Judgement on the value or worth of the activities undertaken up to a particular point in the implementation is made based on comparing the actual changes with the expected results (objectives). The foregoing discourse is a description and explanation of the foundation of ongoing evaluation (and by extrapolation terminal evaluation); all other issues relating to ongoing evaluation are built upon this foundation.

Ongoing evaluation, like monitoring, should be undertaken at predetermined stages of implementation as outlined in the monitoring and evaluation (M&E) plan of the programme document. It provides an early feedback on programme weaknesses, which can be used to modify or adjust the remaining stages of a programme. Thus information provided from evaluations conducted during programme implementation can be used to modify or adjust subsequent stages of a programme. The formulation of evaluation criteria based on programme objectives is just one of the options open to extension organisations and their stakeholders. This approach is in concordance with the *Attainment of Objectives Model* of programme evaluation (Deshler). According to Deshler, the model assumes that the success of a programme can be determined by measuring a programme's outcomes against its own goals and objectives. Thus measurable objectives (as stated in the programme document) are clarified and data are gathered that validate the extent to which these objectives have been met. In ongoing evaluation, this is done at specified stages of implementation as explained above. Ongoing evaluation, if well conducted and applied, contributes immensely to achievement of overall programme objectives and goals.

Terminal evaluation provides a means for a leader to know the extent to which a programme achieved its objectives and/or goals. It is also known as Post-implementation Evaluation, and focuses on examining the overall impact of the programme.

Thus for each type of evaluation – programme appraisal, ongoing evaluation or terminal evaluation – criteria are set, evidences are collected and judgment is passed by comparing the criteria with the evidence. Complex as the evaluation process may appear, a leader needs to undertake it to know the extent to which his targets have been achieved. Just like planning, implementation and monitoring, evaluation is also spearheaded by the leader and he needs to put the proper measures in place to ensure that the process is undertaken and undertaken effectively.

## 3:6 CONCLUDING REMARKS ON LEADERS' FOUR BASIC FUNCTIONS

In this Chapter I have attempted to explain the four basic functions that every leader must perform to ensure effective leadership. Leaders may perform these four functions to varying degrees and extent depending on their skills and the nature of the groups that they lead. It is obvious that the planning, implementation, monitoring and evaluation efforts expected of, say, a Class Captain, would be far less than that expected of a School Prefect. In the same vein, the planning, implementation, monitoring and evaluation efforts expected of, say, District Chief Executive Officer would be far less than that expected of a Regional Minister. Thus what is important is for every leader to be skilful in the performance of the four functions and perform them according to the dictates of the group.

# CHAPTER FOUR

## WHAT DO LEADERS NEED TO PERFORM EFFECTIVELY?

### 4:1 INTRODUCTION

Leadership is obviously an arduous task and leaders, by their strategic position, carry a lot on their shoulders. Leadership is a multitasking role that requires various traits, knowledge, attitude and skills for optimum performance. In this Chapter I present an outline of the traits, knowledge, attitude and skills needed by leaders to perform their four core functions effectively.

### 4:1:1 Leaders need a thorough understanding of themselves

A basic advice for any person in a leadership position who intends to perform effectively is "know yourself". A leader needs to take pains to systematically know his beliefs, values, principles, abilities, deficiencies, strengths, weaknesses, temperament etc. As a friend once put it, "you may think you know yourself until you consciously attempt to find out who you are". There are so many things we assume about ourselves until we take pains to understand them. A leader who knows himself very well stands a better chance of managing himself effectively to the benefit of the group that he leads. He is able to identify aspects of his life that empower the group and vice versa and he is able to identify areas of his life that require change and improvement for the benefit of the group.

An important step to self examination is to embrace criticism. A lot of the times criticisms of our actions give significant indication of our behavior. If we are accommodative enough to examine such criticism in good faith we are likely to gain a better understanding of ourselves. Further to this, and according to the word of God, we can ask God for wisdom to enable us delve deep into ourselves to understand ourselves better. This involves fervent prayer and meditation.

**4:1:2  Leaders need continuous self-improvement**
Groups are dynamic, just as the environment in which they operate. Thus leaders have no choice but to be wise, diligent and intelligent. It is therefore

mandatory that leaders continually improve themselves mentally, physically, spiritually, character-wise, competence-wise, etc. A leader who fails to improve himself in these areas may wake up one day and find himself irrelevant to his group. Self-examination, as was mentioned above, provides the basis for determining areas of a leader's life that need improvement. Also important is a thorough assessment of the leadership roles that provide pointers to the types of training programmes needed by the leader to improve himself.

Formal and informal education are both avenues that a leader can explore to improve himself. The internet has become a very powerful and readily available source of information and leaders need to explore it as they seek information to improve upon their skills. An educated leader (formal, informal or non-formal) is a great assert to himself and the group.

### 4:1:3 Leaders need a good understanding of their groups

Leaders exist to inspire, direct, influence and support a group to achieve the group's goals, objectives and aspirations. To be able to do this effectively, leaders must know and understand their groups thoroughly. This involves knowing and understanding the culture, goals, constitution, resources, needs, challenges, aspirations, skills etc of the group. Indeed a leader must know all there is to know about the group that he leads. A good understanding of the group empowers the leader to use appropriate leadership skills to lead effectively.

This may require an occasional reconnaissance study of the group to update the leader's knowledge of the group. Planning for various projects for the group provides the opportunity for such reconnaissance studies.

### 4:1:4 Leaders need to be knowledgeable about the group's environment

Groups, be it family, community, association, corporate organisation or nation, all operate within environments. A group's environment refers to the social, economic, political, religious, spiritual or physical context within which the group operates. A group's environment impacts on the activities and performance of the group. It is in the interest of a leader to know and understand the nitty-gritty of the environment that his group operates in. This will enable him devise strategies that enable the group to exist in harmony with its environment and ultimately make the best of it.

### 4:1:5   Leaders need to attach importance and seriousness to their leadership role

Leadership is a very important and serious role and any person who occupies a leadership position must appreciate that.  A leader who attaches importance and seriousness to his position and role is likely to be more committed to his task as a leader.  He is also more likely to think deeply about issues concerning the group and also have a visionary disposition. Lastly, it could also activate the spirit of service.  The consequences and ramifications of failed leadership for a group and the leader are usually so grave that it is imperative for a leader to consciously attach importance and seriousness to the role.

### 4:1:6   Leaders need the willingness and ability to sacrifice

Leadership calls for sacrifice.   A sacrifice is basically the performance of an activity without the expectation of a direct benefit or compensation. However, it is important to note that some leadership positions come with commensurate remunerations where leaders are appropriately compensated for their roles and responsibilities. But compensation or no compensation, the spirit of sacrifice is the hallmark of effective leadership. The spirit of sacrifice empowers a leader to go the extra mile to make the difference needed for the group to excel. If you cannot sacrifice your time, money, assets, knowledge, ideas, and skills, then you might as well forget about leading a group.

**4:1:7  Leaders need the courage and ability to delegate, be authoritative or democratic as the situation demands.**

We indicated earlier that leadership comes in various shapes and forms generally referred to as Leadership Style. We also noted that three main styles of leadership can be identified, i.e. authoritarian, participative, and delegation.

In the authoritarian style the leader tells his subordinates what he wants done and how he wants it done, without getting their advice.. It must be pointed out that the authoritarian style excludes yelling, using demeaning language and leading by threats and abuse of power. Such behaviours are abusive and unprofessional. In the participative style of leadership, the leader includes one or more of his subordinates in the decision-making process (determining what to do and how to do it). However, the leader maintains the final decision-making authority. Delegation is the process by which responsibility is transferred to lower levels of the hierarchy. In delegation, a leader is ultimately responsible for the success or failure for the work delegated. Delegation reduces a leader's workload to enable him perform essential functions which otherwise might be delayed. In delegating, a leader must identify a capable person who can deliver/perform the function expected of him/her and be sure that the job being delegated can be performed by the subordinate. He must also show appreciation for successful completion of the job; accept failure and put necessary measures in place to avoid future failure; and avoid excessive delegation of duties out of laziness.

Factors that influence the style to be used include a number of considerations such as: amount of time available; basis of relationship between the leader and subordinates - trust or disrespect; who has the necessary information - you, your employees or both; type of task to be undertaken - is it structured;

or unstructured, complicated or simple; and based on laws or established procedures.

Although most leaders use all 3 styles of leadership, one of them becomes the dominant one. An effective leader is one who is knowledgeable of all three styles of leadership and able to apply a particular style appropriately to any given situation. A leader who is able to do that is said to have leadership skill. Leadership skill therefore refers to the ability of a leader to blend the three leadership styles appropriately in every given situation.

In other words, he delegates when the situation demands delegation, he is authoritative when the situation demands it and seeks consensus when the situation demands contribution of ideas and opinions. The challenge to the leader is to know when to apply a particular leadership style for optimum impact.

### 4:1:8   Leaders need effective communication, negotiation, conflict resolution, and marketing skills

It has been said that communication is the life-wire of a society. This means that a society is likely to suffer, or even die without communication. Families, organisations and associations all thrive on effective communication. Communication is basically the process whereby messages/information is transmitted from a source to a receiver. Indeed, the act of communication is to get a message across to others. Communication is important in a society in many ways including the fact that:

- communication enables us to exchange ideas.

- communication enables us to express our feelings or emotions (fears, joy, sadness, disappointment, gratitude etc) to others.

- communication enables us to let others know our needs and vice-versa.

- communication defines our image.

- communication is a force for change.

Effective communication skill is essential to a leader's success. Acquiring good communication skills enables the leader to exchange information effectively with members of his group and those external to the group. Communication can be verbal or non-verbal. Verbal communication refers to communication that involve the use of words whilst non-verbal communication refers to the use of gestures and symbols. One of the hallmarks of good communication is fluency and eloquence.

A leader needs to appreciate the basic rudiments of communication to enable him use it effectively. Communication is effective when the receiver of a message interprets it exactly as the source intended it. To ensure or achieve effective communication we need to understand the elements of communication and accord them the necessary serious attention. The elements of communication are:

- Source (the person sending the information).
- Message (the information to be sent).
- Channel (the preferred medium of transmission).
- Receiver (the person receiving the information).
- Context, (the situation in which the information is being transmitted).
- Feedback (the response of the receiver to the info received).

Thus, communication involves a *source* that transmits a message through a channel to a receiver within a certain *context* which prompts a response from the receiver known as *feedback*. The source or initiator of communication is very important because he/she needs to carefully create the *message* and use a suitable *channel* to ensure that the *receiver* interprets the message as intended. This requires adequate knowledge and understanding of the receiver (his/her temperament, likes and dislikes, aspirations, background/experiences, desires etc.); and that calls for: excellence, diligence, patience, love, empathy, sympathy, compassion, integrity, dignity, wisdom, humility, circumspection, consciousness, a listening ear, prayer, etc. With the above qualities the source is able to create a message and use a *channel* that is suitable or appropriate to the receiver. This implies that the leader has a great responsibility to ensure effective communication and he could also inspire and train his group members to do same.

A leader must also realise that the world is now in the information age after going through the agricultural and industrial ages. The main engine of this age is information and communications technology (ICT). ICT usually refers to new-generation technologies spawned by the marriage of computers and telecommunications. But it is also the product of the convergence of digital technologies encompassing computers, telecommunications, audio-video and publishing. It covers mobile phones, personal computers, the internet, e-mail, imaging technology, digital video and cable television. ICT types range from web-enabled, network and stand-alone technologies. The effective use of ICT can greatly enhance the leader's communication and thereby his performance as a leader. A typical example is the use of emails and social media such as Facebook, Whatsapp, Telegram etc.

Important offshoots of communication are negotiation, conflict resolution and marketing. These offshoots require basic grounding in effective communication plus some extra specific skills for appropriate impact. Some situations in a group may require negotiations within and outside the group; resolution of conflicts within the group and with persons or groups outside the group; and/ or marketing of the group to others for support or partnership. A leader with skills in these areas who applies them appropriately stands a better chance of leading effectively.

### 4:1:9   Leaders need organisational skills

Organisational skill refers to the ability to determine and provide the capital, materials, equipment and the personnel required by a group to achieve its objectives within a specified period of time. Every aspect of a leader's function requires some form of organisation where the necessary things required for the execution of an activity are made available in timely fashion. In organising his work schedules and activities, a leader needs to learn how to delegate effectively since he may not be able to perform all functions required in organising his work.

### 4:1:10  Leaders need the support of their followers

A leader is no leader without followers. Same is a leader who loses the support of his followers. A leader needs to apply all the skills at his disposal to gain the continuous support of his followers. This condition is guaranteed under a democratic dispensation where leaders are elected by the majority of the group members for a specified tenure. But whether elected or otherwise, a leader needs the support of his followers for effective implementation of his vision for the group. Once a leader's followers support him, they are likely to do their best to ensure the success of the leader.

**4:1:11  A leader needs a high sense of Integrity**

Integrity is one of the traits that are usually touted as needed by a leader to perform effectively; and rightly so because it encompasses several other traits that are all required for effective leadership. Some of the synonyms used for integrity are honesty, uprightness, honour, good character, high morality, and virtues. The rest are decency, truthfulness, trustworthiness, sincerity and fairness. In other words, to describe a leader as a person of integrity is to suggest that he exhibits an appreciable dose of these traits, all of which influence leadership positively.

It is also important to note that the word *integrity* evolved from the Latin adjective *integer,* meaning *whole* or *complete.* In this context, integrity is a person's inner sense of "wholeness" where his actions, behaviour and utterances are consistent with his values, beliefs and faith. In other words, a person may be judged as "having integrity" to the extent that he acts according to the values, beliefs and principles he claims to hold. Where these values, beliefs and principles are generally acceptable to society, such persons are perceived by society as being men of integrity.

To the extent that a leader's integrity creates trust and transparency in a group, it is an attribute that every leader needs for effectiveness.

## 4:1:12 Leaders need a fine balance of "competence" and "good character"

In our contemporary world, leaders increasingly have to deal with challenges that require some technical knowledge and understanding, together with the ability to plan, implement, monitor and evaluate programmes. A leader who is able to do these and succeeds in achieving some positive changes in his group is described as competent. However, in addition to competence, a leader needs a good character to make the positive changes in his group more meaningful, acceptable and more fulfilling to himself, the members of his group and society at large. Character, in very simple terms, is the way a person thinks, feels and behaves. Good character requires that a person exhibits respect, understanding, empathy, and all the attributes that give a human face to everything that he does. Threatening and bullying group members to achieve goals will certainly not be acceptable to them and likely to backfire in the long run.

**4:1:13  Leaders need God**

A leader who aspires to perform effectively beyond the expectations of all and sundry must genuinely desire a relationship with God. I am referring to the God of Abraham, the God of Isaac, the God of Jacob, the God and Father of our Lord Jesus Christ, the alpha and the omega, the creator of heaven and earth. For all those who believe in this God and are in leadership positions or aspire to be, we have no choice but to desire Him in everything that we do. Indeed we cannot do without Him. He holds the key to our success as leaders and therefore we need Him to succeed.

To stress this point further, I recount a few verses in the Bible where Biblical leaders alluded to their need of God in the performance of some specific leadership roles:

*Moses (Exodus 3:1-12)*

*¹Now Moses was tending the flock of Jethro his father-in-law, the priest of Midian, and he led the flock to the far side of the wilderness and came to Horeb, the mountain of God. ² There the angel of the LORD appeared to him in flames of fire from within a bush. Moses saw that though the bush was on fire it did not burn up. ³ So Moses thought,*

*"I will go over and see this strange sight – why the bush does not burn up."*

*⁴ When the LORD saw that he had gone over to look, God called to him from within the bush, "Moses! Moses!"*

*And Moses said, "Here I am."*

*⁵ "Do not come any closer," God said. "Take off your sandals, for the place where you are standing is holy ground." ⁶ Then he said, "I am the God of your father,[a] the God of Abraham, the God of Isaac and the God of Jacob." At this, Moses hid his face, because he was afraid to look at God.*

*⁷ The LORD said, "I have indeed seen the misery of my people in Egypt. I have heard them crying out because of their slave drivers, and I am concerned about their suffering. ⁸ So I have come down to rescue them from the hand of the Egyptians and to bring them up out of that land into a good and spacious land, a land flowing with milk and honey – the home of the Canaanites, Hittites, Amorites, Perizzites, Hivites and Jebusites. ⁹ And now the cry of the Israelites has reached me, and I have seen the way the Egyptians are oppressing them. ¹⁰ So now, go. I am sending you to Pharaoh to bring my people the Israelites out of Egypt."*

*[11] But Moses said to God, "Who am I that I should go to Pharaoh and bring the Israelites out of Egypt?"*

*[12] And God said, "I will be with you. And this will be the sign to you that it is I who have sent you: When you have brought the people out of Egypt, you will worship God on this mountain."*

The reassurance from God that He would be with him calmed Moses' nerves as God commissioned him to lead His children out of Egypt. Without God's assurance, Moses wouldn't have had the confidence to accept the assignment, let alone embark on it. Moses appreciated the power of God and knew that he couldn't do what he had been assigned to do without Him. Indeed, Moses proved himself right because he certainly couldn't have led the children of Israel from Egypt to the brink of the Promised Land without God. Leaders really need God.

### Gideon (Judges 6:1-16;)

*[1] The Israelites did evil in the eyes of the LORD, and for seven years he gave them into the hands of the Midianites. [2] Because the power of Midian was so oppressive, the Israelites prepared shelters for themselves in mountain clefts, caves and strongholds. [3] Whenever the Israelites planted their crops, the Midianites, Amalekites and other*

*eastern peoples invaded the country. ⁴ They camped on the land and ruined the crops all the way to Gaza and did not spare a living thing for Israel, neither sheep nor cattle nor donkeys. ⁵ They came up with their livestock and their tents like swarms of locusts. It was impossible to count them or their camels; they invaded the land to ravage it. ⁶ Midian so impoverished the Israelites that they cried out to the LORD for help.*

*⁷ When the Israelites cried out to the LORD because of Midian, ⁸ he sent them a prophet, who said, "This is what the LORD, the God of Israel, says: I brought you up out of Egypt, out of the land of slavery. ⁹ I rescued you from the hand of the Egyptians. And I delivered you from the hand of all your oppressors; I drove them out before you and gave you their land. ¹⁰ I said to you, 'I am the LORD your God; do not worship the gods of the Amorites, in whose land you live.' But you have not listened to me."*

*¹¹ The angel of the LORD came and sat down under the oak in Ophrah that belonged to Joash the Abiezrite, where his son Gideon was threshing wheat in a winepress to keep it from the Midianites. ¹² When the angel of the LORD appeared to Gideon, he said, "The LORD is with you, mighty warrior."*

*¹³ "Pardon me, my lord," Gideon replied, "but if the LORD*

*is with us, why has all this happened to us? Where are all his wonders that our ancestors told us about when they said, 'Did not the LORD bring us up out of Egypt?' But now the LORD has abandoned us and given us into the hand of Midian."*

*[14] The LORD turned to him and said, "Go in the strength you have and save Israel out of Midian's hand. Am I not sending you?"*

*[15] "Pardon me, my lord," Gideon replied, "but how can I save Israel? My clan is the weakest in Manasseh, and I am the least in my family."*

*[16] The LORD answered, "I will be with you, and you will strike down all the Midianites, leaving none alive."*

Just like Moses, Gideon felt inadequate to undertake the assignment that the almighty God was giving to him. He felt inadequate because his focus was on his own strength. When God assured him that He would be with him he took up the challenge and actually succeeded. God's presence made it possible for Gideon to do what appeared impossible. Leaders need God indeed.

### King David (1 Samuel 30)

¹David and his men reached Ziklag on the third day. Now the Amalekites had raided the Negev and Ziklag. They had attacked Ziklag and burned it, ² and had taken captive the women and everyone else in it, both young and old. They killed none of them, but carried them off as they went on their way.

³ When David and his men reached Ziklag, they found it destroyed by fire and their wives and sons and daughters taken captive. ⁴ So David and his men wept aloud until they had no strength left to weep. ⁵ David's two wives had been captured – Ahinoam of Jezreel and Abigail, the widow of Nabal of Carmel. ⁶ David was greatly distressed because the men were talking of stoning him; each one was bitter in spirit because of his sons and daughters. But David found strength in the LORD his God.

⁷ Then David said to Abiathar the priest, the son of Ahimelek, "Bring me the ephod." Abiathar brought it to him, ⁸ and David inquired of the LORD, "Shall I pursue this raiding party? Will I overtake them?"

"Pursue them," he answered. "You will certainly overtake them and succeed in the rescue."

⁹ David and the six hundred men with him came to the

Besor Valley, where some stayed behind. [10] *Two hundred of them were too exhausted to cross the valley, but David and the other four hundred continued the pursuit.*

[11] *They found an Egyptian in a field and brought him to David. They gave him water to drink and food to eat —* [12] *part of a cake of pressed figs and two cakes of raisins. He ate and was revived, for he had not eaten any food or drunk any water for three days and three nights.*

[13] *David asked him, "Who do you belong to? Where do you come from?"*

*He said, "I am an Egyptian, the slave of an Amalekite. My master abandoned me when I became ill three days ago.* [14] *We raided the Negev of the Kerethites, some territory belonging to Judah and the Negev of Caleb. And we burned Ziklag."*

[15] *David asked him, "Can you lead me down to this raiding party?"*

*He answered, "Swear to me before God that you will not kill me or hand me over to my master, and I will take you down to them."*

[16] *He led David down, and there they were, scattered over the countryside, eating, drinking and reveling because*

*of the great amount of plunder they had taken from the land of the Philistines and from Judah.* [17] *David fought them from dusk until the evening of the next day, and none of them got away, except four hundred young men who rode off on camels and fled.* [18] *David recovered everything the Amalekites had taken, including his two wives.* [19] *Nothing was missing: young or old, boy or girl, plunder or anything else they had taken. David brought everything back.* [20] *He took all the flocks and herds, and his men drove them ahead of the other livestock, saying, "This is David's plunder."*

Here and again, God's presence in David's leadership role made it possible for him to recover everything that the Amalekites took from him. With God all things are possible and every leader who aspires to lead effectively must consciously desire God and make Him the centre of his leadership activities.

# CHAPTER FIVE

## BENEFITS OF EFFECTIVE LEADERSHIP

### 5:1 INTRODUCTION

After outlining the basic functions of a leader and explaining what leaders need to perform effectively, it is important to look at the benefits of effective leadership. As I indicated in an earlier chapter, there is a clear difference between 'Leadership' and 'Effective Leadership', and as I noted, "Leadership points to the incidental performance of various roles and activities by a person or persons occupying leadership positions in a group that may or may not impact positively on the group"; whilst "Effective leadership points to the deliberate performance of roles and activities that result in addressing the aspirations, needs, challenges and problems of a group". The benefits of "Effective Leadership" cannot be overemphasized. In my candid opinion, it is the weakest link in all human development endeavours.

**5:2    BENEFITS OF EFFECTIVE LEADERSHIP**

In this section I outline some of the benefits of "Effective Leadership" to the leader, the group and society as a well.

### 5:2:1   Effective leadership motivates a leader for greater heights

A tried and tested motivator for effective leadership is effective leadership itself.  As a leader puts in the needed effort to lead effectively, his achievements propel him to do more as a leader.  The personal satisfaction that he receives from his achievements motivates him to look for more innovative ways to lead effectively.  So if you want to lead effectively, start doing what it takes to become an effective leader and you shall get to the point where effective leadership becomes a second nature.

### 5:2:2   Effective leadership ensures the survival, growth and development of groups

Groups survive, grow and develop through the fulfillment of their needs, aspirations, vision and goals.  Effective leadership ensures that all these are achieved to ensure the survival, growth and development of the group.  Among others, effective leadership ensures that the needs and aspirations of the group are clearly identified and appropriate steps taken to meet those needs and aspirations. Within the same context, effective leadership thinks far into the future to identify things that need to be initiated now to forestall future challenges. It may also call for managing the expectations of members of the group vis-à-vis the possibilities on the ground. All these call for effective planning, implementation, monitoring and evaluation, all of which is a hallmark of effective leadership.

Group members naturally look up to leaders for guidance, direction and inspiration and the only way to satisfy this expectation is through effective leadership.

### 5:2:3   Effective leadership promotes joy, peace and harmony in groups

When leaders are transparent and accountable to their members; when leaders perform their leadership roles with integrity and respect for members; and indeed, when leaders meet the needs and aspirations of the group, the obvious consequence is joy, peace and harmony. Effective leadership may not necessarily rule out misunderstanding, chaos or confusion in a group since human institutions are naturally prone to such negative occurrences, but it has the power to minimize or manage them within acceptable limits.

### 5:2:4 Effective leadership provides a light for followers

I alluded in an earlier Chapter that every person has the potential to lead. In that context, every member of a group is a leader-in-waiting. For all leaders-in-waiting, effective leadership provides a positive learning experience that empowers them to take up the mantle when the opportunity comes. Beyond performing leadership roles in future, effective leadership also serves as a mentorship platform for followers to learn some life skills from their leaders. The point is that effective leadership is a lifestyle of excellence and with the right relationship with a leader, a member of the group can be empowered to excel in life.

### 5:2:5 Effective Leadership builds confidence in people

One of the surest ways to build the confidence of people in their leader is through effective leadership. An effective leader does not need to convince his members to have confidence in him. His works shall speak for themselves and that translate naturally into the group members' confidence in him. That confidence also pays off in providing the leader the necessary support needed to lead the group.

### 5:2:6   Effective leadership has divine rewards

The God of Abraham, the God of Isaac, the God of Jacob, the God and Father of our Lord Jesus is a God of excellence (Psalm 8:1). As his children created in His image it is normal to be a living testimony of His traits, one of which is excellence. Effective leadership provides us the opportunity to exhibit excellence in line with God's excellence trait. Thus every time we exhibit effective leadership, we are actually ministering to somebody about God's excellence and that comes with divine rewards.

# CHAPTER SIX

## LEADERSHIP EXPERIENCES

### 6:1    INTRODUCTION

As indicated in the first chapter, the bulk of the content of this book was written based on my practical experiences with leadership at various levels and in various organizational/institutional setups. As the saying goes, "experience is the best teacher", and indeed, my stints at leadership in those varying capacities created a unique opportunity for me to learn, understand and develop a concept of leadership which I have shared in the earlier chapters of this book.  I have termed this concept of leadership "Functional Leadership", where the focus of leadership is simply the performance of basic leadership functions enabled by time tested leadership traits.

### 6:2    VARIOUS STINTS AT LEADERSHIP

In this section, I present some of my leadership experiences with you.  It is carefully structured, albeit chronologically, to project various leadership traits and performance of leadership functions in real life situations. It also highlights some of my failures and successes as a leader.

### 6:2:1 Leadership Role as Sports Prefect at St. Augustine's College

The first official leadership position that I occupied was the Sports Prefect position at St Augustine's College for the 1985/1986 academic year. The Sports Prefect position was one of seven student leadership positions instituted by the school to support the administration of the school. The others were School Prefect (with two Assistants), Dining Hall Prefect, Entertainment Prefect, Chapel Prefect, Health Prefect and House Prefect (one for each of the ten houses).

For the Sports Prefect position, three other candidates and I expressed interest and we were screened by the prefect body. I emerged as the most suitable candidate from the screening and was recommended to the school authorities who eventually appointed me as the Sports Prefect. On hindsight I must admit that I did not appreciate nor situate my position as a Sports Prefect within the broader context and concept of leadership. Indeed, my utmost desire at the time was to join the prefect body whose role and privileges I had always admired. Being a sportsman myself, the Sports Prefect position seemed the most appropriate hence my decision to stand for the position. From my present understanding of leadership, my closest link with any of the attributes of leadership at the time was my quest to host and win the Cape-Coast annual inter-secondary schools athletics competition for that year. This quest empowered me to work very hard and indeed St. Augustine's College successfully hosted and won the 1985 "Interco", the preferred name for the annual inter-secondary schools athletics competition.

In performing my role as a Sports Prefect, I attended all meetings of the prefect body chaired by my housemate, friend and School Prefect, Ben Nunoo-Mensah. I also helped to maintain order and good behaviour among students on campus in general; helped to maintain order in the dining hall; read announcements during dining, and helped to maintain discipline during evening "prep" when students gathered to learn in their various classrooms. I also mentored some students. As a member of the student body I served as a link between students and the school authorities. I also represented the school, together with other prefects at programmes outside the school. In relation to sports specifically, I organised the juniors to prepare the Augusco Stadium for the "Interco" event and partnered the Sports Master to prepare our athletes for the "Interco" which eventually paid back with Augusco winning the trophy.

Once again I want to emphasise that in playing my role as a Sports Prefect I had no inkling of leadership as a concept; I presented myself for a position and I was determined to do everything possible to vindicate myself. Now I know that I was exhibiting some critical traits of leadership, including commitment, quest for success, hard work, and organisation.

An exciting leadership role that I performed during my stewardship as Sports Prefect was the role of an "Operations Commander" in a mock coup plot at Augusco. This event is well captured in my midlife autobiography, "Adventures Beyond Mpataba: Reconciling with God". As I indicated in that book, "My experience as the operations commander brought to the fore some essential personal traits such as organisational ability, respect for time, trust in my instinct, loyalty, respect for authority, confidentiality, confidence and humility". Now I know that these are all traits that are essential for leadership and every leader must yearn for them.

## 6:2:2   Leadership role as Head of Ackah-Nyamike Jnr. Family

My next major stint with leadership after leaving Augusco was my position and role as head of the Ackah-Nyamike Jnr. Family.    This leadership role began with a traditional marriage which was subsequently blessed with two wonderful boys.  A leader, as I indicated earlier on in this book, is a person who provides support, guidance and direction to a group of people to achieve their goals and vision. Thus I became a leader of the Ackah-Nyamike Jnr. Family when I married and had children as well.  In my new position as a husband and father I needed to provide support, guidance and direction to my wife and children to achieve commonly acceptable goals and vision of a family such as love, peace and joy; spiritual growth; food, accommodation and clothing for the family; financial independence; education for children; health for the family; and social networking among others.

Due to circumstances which at the time appeared beyond my control, the six year old marriage ended in divorce. As the leader of that family unit I take full responsibility for the failure in line with my current understanding of leadership. This is without prejudice to my personal assessment of the causes of the failure which pointed to poor pre-marital preparation.

I received another chance at leadership of a complete nuclear family when I remarried in the year 2001. With a better pre-marital preparation and a better understanding of marriage I can say with confidence that "so far so good", even though there is room for improvement. In my quest to lead effectively I continue to provide support, guidance, and help to all members of the nuclear Ackah-Nyamike Jnr. Family made up of my wife, five biological children (Derrick, Dennis, Yaba, Akasi, and Immanuel) and an unofficially adopted child, Sarah.

Being an informal institution, leadership at the family level, especially the nuclear family level is equally very informal without structures or clear laid out procedures or processes. However, there are some principles that have been helpful as I provide leadership for my nuclear family:

- ✓ Education is key to freedom – education of the children is top priority for me. At the time of writing this book, my eldest son had completed his Bachelor of Law programme at University of Ghana, Legon; my second son was in the second year of his three year Senior High School programme at St. Augustine's College, Cape Coast; the last three are at JHS 3, Class 6 and kindergarten respectively at Christ the King International School, Cantonments, Accra. By the Grace of God and by our genuine interest in their education they are all performing above average.

- ✓ Integrity, discipline, and hard work are indispensible traits. Through acts of correction, encouragement, sanctions and rewards, the children have become conscious of integrity, discipline and hard work and do their best to live by them albeit with challenges.

- ✓ Spare the rod and spoil the child – my rod here is verbal intervention.

- ✓ Everything in the physical realm has roots in the spiritual realm – relationship with God is paramount. I continue to do my best as the leader of the family to establish the family members firmly in the Word of God through attendance at church, teachings and other spiritual exercises including prayer and fasting.

✓ Excellence must be pursued in all things. This is very well known to them because I demand excellence in every little thing that they do.

✓ Respect is mutual – respect the children and they will respect you in return.

✓ Leadership by example – action speaks louder than words.

✓ The spoken word is very powerful – mind what you say.

✓ Train up a child in the way he should go: and when he is old he will not depart from it.

The above principles have been a great guide in my leadership role as the head of the Ackah-Nyamike Jnr. Family unit. The response of my wife and children to my leadership role has been positive and productive. As far as my physical and spiritual eyes can see, the principles outlined above are shaping their lives and there is appreciable peace and harmony at home. Indeed the group (Ackah-Nyamike Jnr. Family) is achieving its goals and vision day in day out under my humble leadership.

### 6:2:3 Leadership role as Head of Ackah-Eyepa Abozoama

My late father was one of four children born to my grandmother Mame Ena and Grandfather, Ackah-Eyepa. All four of them, made up of three males and a female, gave birth to various numbers of children totaling twenty-five, three of whom have gone to be with the Lord. In the Nzema tribe which we belong to, cousins are considered as siblings. Coincidentally our parents died according to their ages, starting from the eldest to the youngest. A couple of years after the death of our last parent I proposed the formation of a group to bring together all 22 surviving children of our four parents. The objective of the group as I perceived it at the time was to create a platform to present a united front as far as issues concerning us were concerned and also to support members of the group during times of need. At the time of setting up the group, three of the twenty two children were living abroad, twelve were resident in Accra and the rest were resident in Allowuley.

To set the group formation in motion we arranged for a meeting at Allowuley which was well attended. Unfortunately I could not attend the maiden meeting due to circumstances beyond my control. However by unanimous decision I was acknowledged as official head of the group while the only surviving son of the only lady among our parents was acknowledged as the traditional head. My younger brother, BB, serves as the scribe of the group. The group members also came up with "Ackah-Eyepa Abozoama" as the name for the group. This name sought to give an indication that we are descendants of Egya Ackah-Eyepa, our grandfather.

As leader of the group I arranged subsequent meetings one of which was held in Accra. Under my leadership the group continues to support members as and when the situation demands. We have been able to set up an investment fund which members contribute into monthly. We have also been able to secure and obtain documents for a sizeable piece of farming land which our parents left for us. According to some members of the group, my quest for unity, trustworthiness and respect for all have been instrumental in keeping the group together.

Even though some apathy has crept into the group due to petty bickering among members back home in the village, the group is still in shape with the Accra Chapter being strong as ever. I guess it is part of my role as the leader to address these bickerings to enhance unity among all members.

### 6:2:4 Leadership Role as General Secretary of Allowuley Citizens Association

I noted in my Autobiography that I am a full blooded Nzema who hails from a town called Allowuley on my paternal side and from Bamiankor, Tikobo 2, Eikwe and Mpataba on my maternal side. Due to an arrangement that my father put in place for my siblings and I to visit Allowuley during our primary school vacations I got bonded to the town and developed an interest in their growth and development whilst I was growing up.

Allowuley is a steadily expanding town with a population in excess of 3,000 made up of about 300 households. Despite its relative small size, it is the custodian of a large tract of land stretching across a number of towns. When I returned from the United Kingdom after the completion of my PhD, I decided to participate actively in the development affairs of the town. The first step I took was to strengthen the Allowuley Citizens Association in Accra through which I was elected the General Secretary. As the General Secretary of the Association I spearheaded a review of the Association's constitution to make it more meaningful to its members and to the development of Allowuley. I whipped up the interest of the members in the activities of the Association through the promotion of issue-based meetings and attractive social programmes. As part of the Association's rejuvenation process it was re-launched in Allowuley in July 2005 to coincide with the first anniversary of the death of my father as a memorial and honour to him.

The re-launch of the Allowuley Citizens' Association was attended by the Member of Parliament for the area (Honourable Lee Ocran), the Jomoro District Chief Executive (Mr. Martin Nyameke Ackah), the head of the Catholic diocese in the area and other dignitaries. Prior to the re-launch of the Association at Allowuley, I arranged for our Organising Secretary, Mr. Joseph Ewulley, and an elder of Allowuley, Mr. Patrick Cudjoe to appear on the Nzema segment of GTV's Breakfast Show. They discussed the relevance of the association to the development of Allowuley and neighbouring towns with Mr. Atobora Akye, the host of the programme. In August 2007, under the auspices of the Allowuley Citizens Association, I launched the Ackah-Nyamike Students Awards Scheme where deserving students of the town's Junior High School received various awards. Almost every able-bodied person in the town attended the maiden awards ceremony. Due to some circumstances beyond my control, the scheme has been on hold for a while.

To determine intervention areas for the sustainable development of Allowuley I designed and undertook a baseline survey of the town. I sought the consent of the traditional authority before undertaking the survey. I had observed through cursory social investigations that the joint efforts of the Central Government, the Jomoro District Assembly, the Traditional Leaders, Community Members, the Allowuley Citizens Association in Accra, and other benevolent people had made it possible for the town to have access to electricity supply, drinking water, public toilet facility and communication facilities including telephone services. But aside from the above accomplishments, the town had not made significant headway in the provision of good basic education for its children, the expansion of employment opportunities and improvement in existing ones, the creation of awareness and provision of education on HIV/AIDS and other infectious diseases, the control and/or prevention of environmental degradation, especially erosion, and instilling communal spirit in the people, among others.

I had also observed that the prospect of achieving significant improvements in the areas stated above was made less likely by the apparent ineptitude of the town's traditional leaders, who, together with agents of the Jomoro District Assembly are responsible for spearheading the town's development efforts. The rapid expansion and increasing population of the town, added to the complexity of the developmental problems.   The baseline survey was therefore conducted to obtain information to help address the situation.  Although the use of the baseline survey results for the development of the town has been slower than I intended, the plan is still on course and I believe God will continue to grant me the grace to contribute my quota to the development of Allowuley.   Furthermore, the Association's buoyancy experienced a nosedive following the death of one of the prominent members of the Association. All attempts to revive the Association has been unsuccessful so far, albeit I must admit that the effort at reviving the association has not been that strong or persistent.

## 6:2:5 Leadership Role as Head of Department of Agricultural Extension, University of Ghana, Legon

One of the most challenging but equally rewarding leadership role that I ever played was my role as Head of the Department of Agricultural Extension, University of Ghana, Legon. Upon my return to Ghana from Reading University, UK, after the completion of my PhD, I resumed lecturing in the department in the first semester of the 2004/2005 academic year. In July 2005 the Vice-Chancellor, following consultations and on the recommendation of the Acting Dean of the School of Agriculture, appointed me Head of the Department of Agricultural Extension for a two-year term running from 1 August 2005 to 31 July 2007. This was renewed in July 2007 for another two years from 1 August 2007 to 31 July 2009.

Taking over from Dr. F.Y.M Fiadjoe who was due for retirement, I assumed leadership of the department and set myself to contribute my quota to the development of a department which I had been associated with since 1990.

My duties as Head of Department as contained in my appointment letter included:

- Providing leadership and promoting efficiency and good order in the department;
- Meeting members of the department to discuss the mission/vision statement and plans for fulfilling the statement;
- Organising the teaching and research programmes of the department;
- Maintaining acceptable standards of teaching and any other academic work;
- Providing for the examination of students, and ensuring that examinations are promptly processed and results declared in good time;
- Ensuring that research is carried out;
- Advancing and promoting the well being of the department; and
- Carrying out any other duties that may be assigned by the Vice-Chancellor

In line with the university's policy, I attended a one-week workshop organised by the university for newly appointed Heads of Department. We were taken through various topics including: Academic Leadership at the Departmental Level; Appointments and Promotion; Conduct of Meetings; and Effective Teaching and Learning. The rest were 'Grantsmanship'; ICT for Teaching, Learning and Management; and Leadership – Achieving Results through People and Resource Management. Armed with the knowledge from the workshop, I conducted my headship duties to the best of my ability.

By that appointment I became an automatic member of the following boards: the Academic Board of the University; the Board of the College of Agriculture and Consumer Sciences; and the Board of the School of Agriculture. The Board of the College of Agriculture and Consumer Sciences also appointed me to serve as their representative on the Board of Research and Graduate Studies, and the Inter-Faculty Appointments Review Committee for the College of Agriculture and Consumer Sciences. My membership of the above boards and committee greatly enriched my knowledge and understanding of the university system and gave me an opportunity to contribute to the growth and development of the University. I attended all meetings with an open mind and contributed objectively and constructively to all discussions.

In addition to regular attendance at Board and Committee meetings, I also had administrative duties in my department to contend with. I chaired meetings of staff, senior members, as well as student consultative meetings in the department and exercised oversight responsibilities for examinations, teaching, research and extension. As part of my duties I also perused all letters addressed to the department and responded appropriately. Although I had a hardworking secretary, a very loyal typist and a competent office clerk/messenger to support me, I still participated actively in all aspects of the department's work such as typing, occasional filing of official letters, inviting and chasing artisans to undertake repairs and maintenance works, requesting pro-forma invoices, and purchasing equipment and materials. I did all these because I always felt I had to support the staff to ensure that the department's work was done to perfection.

My style of leadership was largely participatory, interspersed with authoritative and delegation styles.

I received an appreciable level of cooperation from my colleagues probably because I did not give them cause to rebel or oppose me unnecessarily. They were very open with me and we discussed issues as colleagues. When they were uncomfortable with my decisions, they never hesitated to come to me for clarifications. During my term as Head, I facilitated the appointment of Dr. (Mrs.) Comfort Freeman as a lecturer in the department, and she became the only female lecturer in the department. After my resignation in 2009, another female was appointed as a lecturer in the department. This is very important for a department that has been dominated by male lecturers for most part of its existence.

My official interaction with students as Head of Department was mainly with the Department's postgraduate students. I had a fruitful relationship with them as Head of Department and was privileged to receive a citation from the 2006-2008 M.Phil. class which read as follows:

*"The very first time we met, you made us feel at home. You treated us as though we were already part of this wonderful department. You have made our stay in the Department of Agricultural Extension a comfortable and a happy one. Dr. Edward Ackah-Nyamike Jnr. You are*

*more than a Head of Department; you are a true leader.*
*We shall always be grateful. God richly bless you!!!"*

I also had a fruitful relationship with the leadership
of the undergraduate students. In recognition of
this relationship, the Legon Branch of the Ghana
Association of Agricultural Students (G.A.A.S.)
presented me with a Citation of Recognition
during their 2007/2008 end-of-year dinner with the
following words:

*"It seems almost superfluous to say how delightful we*
*are for your kind support, advice, time, commitment, and*
*above all moral support for the success of this 2007/2008*
*administration. In fact, you were a father to us and your*
*works will never be deleted from our memories. We thank*
*the Almighty God for your life. May you live long to enjoy*
*the fruits of your labour. May God grant you strength*
*and prosperity to continue to support the activities of*
*GAAS. May your love for GAAS never dwindle; may it*
*increase from strength to strength. Above all, may you*
*continue to be a blessing and a vessel of honour to the*
*people around you. May they find peace in your bosom.*
*God richly bless you"*

One of the highlights of my tenure as Head of
Department was when I served as the Secretary to the

Search Committee for Registrar that recommended the current Registrar of the University of Ghana, Mr J.S. Budu, for appointment. The Committee which was chaired by His Lordship Justice S.K. Date-Bah (Supreme Court Judge and current chairman of Council, University of Ghana) had other members as Professor W. S. Alhassan, Mr. K. Mensa-Bonsu and Mr. Samuel Ofori-Adjei, representing Council of the University, and Prof. Bruce Banoeng-Yakubo, Prof. Ernest Aryeetey (current Vice-Chancellor of the University of Ghana), and Professor Yaa Ntiamoa representing the Academic Board. Although it was my very first time of playing such a role at that high profile level, I did it to the best of my ability and our report was accepted without any reservations. Subsequently I also served on a Board in 2009 that assessed the application for renewal of appointment of the then Dean of the Faculty of Science. The Board was chaired by Professor Emeritus E. Laing.

## 6:2:6  Leadership Role as Patron of Legon Branch of the National Association of Action Students

I fellowshipped with Archbishop Duncan Williams' Action Chapel International from 2005 to 2011 as part of my spiritual growth process. During that period I served the church in various capacities such as: member of the Protocol Department; member of Council of the Dominion University College, an educational wing of the Church; member of the Action Scholarship Board; and Patron of the National Association of Action Students (NAAS) of the Duncan Williams Campus Ministry on Legon Campus.

In recognition of their appreciation for my support to them, the executives of the Legon Branch of NAAS, led by Wilhelmina Parker, wrote the following about me in a citation:

*"His every step speaks humility, boldness and courage. You speak and every word that proceeds out of your lips of clay brings the fullness of joy. Like an apple tree among the trees of the wood, so are you among the great brains. You set your mind on good and Godly things. You commit yourself to making sure they come to pass. Surely you will go places because the road leading to greatness is laid gloriously before you. Campus Ministry is blessed to have you. We love you and therefore say, this is just the beginning of your greatness. Oh man of God! How blessed are those who find themselves caught up in your web of wisdom. We are highly honoured to be connected to such a great personality of your calibre. May the eyes*

*of the Lord not lose sight of you! May His rod of comfort direct you to the destination of His perfect will for your life"*

### 6:2:7 Leadership Role as Convenor, 1984 Year Group of St Augustine's College Past Students Union (APSU '84)

In the year 2005 members of APSU 84 based in Accra elected me to lead the group. At the time the group had about twenty five dedicated members in Accra who had kept the group intact for almost fifteen years from its formation. Subsequently branches of the group were formed in the UK and USA and both branches as well as members scattered in Ghana and other countries all acknowledged me as their leader since Accra is considered the headquarters.

As Convenor of the year group, I chaired all meetings and also represented the year group on the National Executive Council of the St. Augustine's Past Students Union. Together with my executive members we administered the year group effectively.

In March 2009 I led the year group to play a significant role in the organisation of a grand 79th Speech and Prize Giving Day for St. Augustine's College. Our direct involvement in the organisation of the 79th Speech and Prize Giving Day was in line with the APSU National body's arrangement with the College to allow the various year groups to assist directly in the organisation of the College's annual speech and prize-giving day 25 years after leaving the college. And to commemorate 25 years of leaving Augusco we (APSU '84) built a Gatehouse which was commissioned at the 79th Speech and Prize-Giving Day of the school. I also had the pleasure and honour to chair that particular Speech and Prize-Giving Day which was attended by renowned members of APSU, parents and teachers and the general public. APSU '84 continues to support the school which has contributed so much to what we are today.

After commemorating that memorable speech day and upon the persistent advice of a member of the year group I spearheaded the formation of an investment club for interested members of the group in the year 2012. As at the time of writing this book the investment club's portfolio was in excess of fifty thousand Ghana cedis (GHS50,000). To catch up with communication technology advancement, a whatsapp platform was also created for the group which made it possible over a short period to reunite over one hundred members of the group in Austria, Ghana, UK, USA, Canada, and China.

The unity in the group keeps growing stronger and stronger mostly due to very dedicated and committed members as well as my effective leadership.

## 6:2:8   Leadership Role as Managing Director of Venaco Lodge Limited

One of the businesses that my parents established in their quest to diversify their sources of income was a hotel business which they named Venaco Lodge, located at North Kaneshie, near St. Teresa's School. It is very close to the North Kaneshie Branch of Barclays Bank and shares a wall with the North Kaneshie Post Office. A year before my appointment as lecturer with University of Ghana, Legon in 1996, I spearheaded the reopening of the hotel after a long recess spanning from the early 1980s. I managed the hotel till 1999 when I left for UK to study for my PhD programme. When I finally returned to Ghana in 2004, I resumed management of the hotel partially until my resignation from the University in 2009 when I took full control of the business.

Venaco Lodge is a Budget hotel with ten rooms, a bar, a restaurant and a spacious parking space. In line with general hotel management principles I structured the operations of Venaco Lodge to capture units such as: Front Desk (Reception); House Keeping; Laundry Services; General Cleaning; Security; and Bar and Restaurant. As and when needed I interview and employ workers to occupy positions in the various units. I am also assisted by a secretary who augments my duties at the Lodge and other duties under the "Office of Dr. Ackah-Nyamike Jnr".

Over the years the hotel has met its statutory obligations in relation to Insurance Policy for the hotel building; submission of Annual Returns to Registrar General's Department; SSNIT Registration and regular payments for staff; Successful migration from SSNIT Tier 2 to Axis Pension Scheme Tier 2 and up-to-date payment of all staff contributions; Payment of staff's P.A.Y.E to Ghana Revenue Authority; payment of all tax obligations, including VAT and Company Tax; Payment of annual property rates; Payment of annual Business Operating Permits; Successful acquisition of Food Hygiene Certificate from Food & Drugs Authority for the operation of a restaurant; Acquisition of Fire Certificate; and Acquisition of Environmental Protection Agency Licence.

I have also put in place a well structured hotel management system for the smooth running of the hotel. I adhered to basic leadership functions at the hotel by planning, implementating, monitoring and evaluating all activities. Relationship with staff is great and the lodge enjoys appreciable patronage from clients due to satisfactory facilities and customer services. One area of the business that I believe I have not performed well is in the area of expansion. By simple business projection, Venaco Lodge should have expanded from the current ten rooms to about fifty or more rooms. But once I still have life, there is great opportunity to carry out that expansion.

### 6:2:9   Leadership Role as Founder and President of CORD Family International

In line with a renewed commitment to walk effectively with the Almighty God after an encounter with His Word in November 2004, and by inspiration of the Holy Spirit, I founded a Christian non-denominational organization in November 2010 which I named CORD Family International (CFI). CFI was registered at the Registrar General's Department in November 2010 as a company limited by guarantee. 'CORD' is an acronym that stands for Consistency, Obedience, Reverence, and Discipline in relation to our walk with the Almighty God. Consistency builds our faith; obedience yields us His blessings; reverence glorifies Him and discipline keeps us under His care.

In January 2011 I set up a five-member Management Team in line with the proposed organisational structure for CFI. The members of the team were my wife, Mrs Juliet Ackah-Nyamike, Mrs Charity Dodoo, Ms. Winifred Osei, Mr. Ralph Nii Armah and my humble self. Our meetings were held once every month.

With the assistance of the CFI Management Team we launched the organisation on Saturday 10 December 2011 at G.S Plaza Hotel, South Legon. The guest speaker for the occasion was Mr. Albert Ocran a renowned motivational speaker and award winning author. The guests were welcomed by Dr. Kwesi Appiah and the launch itself was performed by Rev. Jonas Koranteng-Smart of Action Chapel International. Other special guests at the launch were Prof. Ben Ahunu, former Provost of College of Agriculture and Consumer Sciences, Mrs Yaa Boatemaa Asiedu, C.E.O. of Ruack Couture Institute,

Pastor Nana Kwame Opoku and Mr. Johnny Watson, C.E.O. of Mayfair Estates Ltd. My siblings, in-laws, friends and some of my former students participated in the launch.

The Vision of CFI is to become *"a vibrant global Christian interdenominational organization that is in close communion with the Holy Spirit, has Jesus Christ at the centre of its affairs, and is a living testimony to the attributes of God.* The mission of The Family is "to empower members of The Family, and the global Christian community at large, through mentoring, training, counselling, guidance, and other support services that enables them to experience an effective and fruitful walk with God and thereby overcome the world". The aims of the CFI are:

(a) To reach out to the general public with the Word of God.

(b) To testify to God's attributes (love, power, grace, faithfulness, wisdom, excellence, etc).

(c) To promote and enhance an effective walk with God among the members of The Family.

(d) To promote the practice of the principles of consistency, obedience, reverence and discipline among members.

(e) To support members of The Family in ways

that shall make them productive.

(f) To organize activities aimed at the general welfare of members of The Family.

(g) To create and facilitate a spiritual, economic and social network among the members of The Family.

(h) To impact society positively and to create a better world through services offered to members and the global Christian community.

Membership of CFI is by appointment as recommended by the Management Team and approved by the Family's Board. Persons qualified to be appointed as members are male and female Christian students of recognized educational institutions aged between 15 and 35. Such appointed persons are known as CFI Ambassadors. Upon completion of their education in their respective institutions, the CFI ambassadors are inducted, if they are willing, as full members of the family with defined roles. The Family also admits persons of high social and spiritual standing aged 35 years and above as Associate Members.

The responsibilities of CFI Ambassadors include, but not limited to:

i. Represent CFI in their respective educational institutions.

ii. Promote the vision, mission and principles of CFI in their respective educational institutions.

iii. Submit applications for support to CFI on behalf of students in their respective educational institutions who genuinely need the support.

iv. Undertake specific activities as directed by CFI leadership.

v. Present term or semester reports on CFI activities undertaken in their respective educational institutions.

CFI Ambassadors receive several benefits including:

(a) Spiritual, economical and social development.

(b) Sense of belonging.

(c) Regular encouragement in walk with God.

(d) Access to mentorship, counselling, training and other support services for spiritual and economic growth.

(e) Access to regular intercessory prayers from the Family's Prayer Team.

(f) Opportunities to be of service to others.

(g) Social, spiritual and economic networking.

(h) Transformed lives through the transforming power of the Holy Spirit.

CORD Family International is governed by a three tier organizational structure made up of an Operations Team, a Management Team and a Family Board. The day-to-day running of The Family is undertaken by a body known as the CORD Family Operations Team made up of two persons. Members of the Operations Team are appointed by the Family Board in consultation with the Management Team. The Operations Team is responsible for planning and implementation of CORD Family activities in line with its Vision and Mission and as outlined in the Family's Operations Manual. The CORD Family Operations Team presents a monthly report of its activities at the monthly meetings of the CORD Family Management Team. The CORD Family Operations Team also prepares a Performance Report (Terminal Evaluation Report) of its activities in a particular year.

The CORD Family Management Team provides direction to the Operations Team. Members of the CORD Family Management Team comprise the Vice-President as chairperson, the leader of the Operations Team, and three other members appointed by the Family Board. Members of the CORD Family Management Team meet once a month (except January).

The supreme authority of The Family is vested in a five-member body known as the CORD Family Board. The five-member CORD Family Board comprises the President of The Family, the Vice-President of The Family, and three other persons appointed by the President in consultation with the Vice-President. The CORD Family Board provides leadership, funding, policy formulation, general guidance and supervision, to the Management and Operation Teams of The Family to ensure the achievement of its Vision, Mission and Aims. The CORD Family Board oversees all activities of The Family as undertaken by the Management and Operation Teams. The President presides over all meetings of the CORD Family Board. The Vice-President assists the President in the performance of his duties and act as President in his absence.

The official activities of the Family are undertaken at an office known as the CORD Family Administrative Office. The CORD Family Administrative Office is run by an Administrative Officer appointed by the Family Board on recommendation by the Management Team. The administrative office operates on a budget prepared and submitted by the Administrative Officer through the Operations Manager to the Management Team for approval.

The responsibilities of the Administrative Officer include:

i.    Responsible for the day-to-day running of the office

ii.    Manage the office's stationery such as purchasing and supply of same to the team members

iii.    Ensure that the office is clean and tidy at all times

iv.    Ensure that utility bills of the office are settled promptly (electricity, telephone, internet etc)

v.    Ensure that all electronic and other equipment in the office are functional and effective

vi.    Carry out general administrative and office managerial tasks including typing, filing, telephone answering, data entry, record keeping, printing, binding, photocopying, scanning, internet surfing etc

vii.    Deal with public and members' enquiries about the Family via phone, email and face-to-face contact at the CORD Family office

viii.  Book appointments on behalf of the teams

ix.  Provide secretarial support to the Operations Team

x.  Receive guests at the office

xi.  Schedule leave arrangements for the Operations Team

xii.  Keep an office attendance book for office staff

xiii.  Operate an 'Accountable Imprest' and 'Book Keeping' for all monetary transactions at the office

xiv.  Conduct literature review (including web-based research) as requested by the Operations Team

xv.  Report writing

Members of The Family meet once a year in December in the form of a Family Conference. New members are inducted at such Annual Family Conferences. The President presents the state of the Family to members of The Family at the Annual Family Conference. Leading CFI has been quite exciting for me as I reach deep into my leadership skills and qualities to grow and develop the Family. Apart from funding which continue to restrict the scale of operations of the

Family, all is going well and the Vision is on course.

### 6:2:10 Leadership Roles as Secretary, and Vice-President of Beautifulgate Chapter (FGBMFI)

I joined the Full Gospel Business Men's Fellowship International (FGBMFI) in 2011 after Dr. Kwesi Appiah (my senior at St Georges House, St. Augustine's College) convinced me to join him and other friends to establish a new Chapter of the Fellowship at G.S. Plaza Hotel, near the Tetteh Quarshie Interchange, South Legon. I was appointed as the Interim Secretary of the Chapter and subsequently elected as the substantive Chapter Secretary. Together with other executives of the Chapter we worked very hard and got the Chapter inaugurated on 21 April 2012.

As Chapter Secretary I participated in all meetings of the Executive Committee of the Chapter and also undertook duties including:
- ✓ Compiling attendance list at our weekly Tuesday meetings.
- ✓ Compiling attendance list at Breakfast meetings held every third Saturday of a month.

✓ Writing minutes of Business Meetings and Chapter Executive meetings.

✓ Informing Chapter members of all meetings – Tuesdays and Breakfast meetings – mostly through SMS and occasionally through phone calls.

✓ Compiling Chapter monthly report and submission of same to Chapter Treasurer for further action to the Chapter President.

✓ Writing invitation letters to Speakers for Tuesday and Breakfast meetings.

✓ Signatory to the Chapter's cheque book; requesting for monthly bank statements and submitting same to the Treasurer for compilation of monthly reports; plus other correspondences with the bank.

✓ Preparation and Printing of Breakfast meeting brochure.

In line with communication technology advancement, I created and administer whatsapp platforms for the Chapter Members and Executives which has enhanced communication in the chapter tremendously. The members' whatsapp platform is also used to share the word of God daily by members.

Beyond these basic secretarial activities I participate in all activities of the Chapter including leading Bible studies on various topics. Some of the teachings and seminars that I have presented at the Chapter were on topics such as: Bargaining with God; Effective Communication; Healing People Healing Nations; Leadership Demystified; and Mind of Christ. The rest are Presumptuous Sins; Testing and Trials; The Believer's Attitude; The Will of God; A Biblical Perspective of Corruption; and a Spiritual Perspective of Addiction.

As a Chapter Executive I have also had the opportunity to share my life testimony as a Main Speaker at a number of Chapters including my own Chapter, Beautiful Gate Chapter; East Legon Chapter; Young Executive Chapter; Winneba Chapter; GREDA Chapter; Pokuase Chapter; Kantamanto Chapter; and Spring Gate Chapter.

I served as Chapter Secretary for Beautifulgate Chapter from 2012 till October 2015 when I was elected Vice-President of the Chapter. As Vice-President I assist the President and other executives to administer the Chapter through planning, implementation, monitoring and evaluation.

## 6:2:11 Chairman, Greater Accra Regional Branch of Ghana Hotels Association.

Venaco Lodge Ltd., where I serve as Managing Director, joined the Ghana Hotels Association (GHA) in 1998 after receiving an operational license from the then Ghana Tourism Board (now Ghana Tourism Authority) to operate as a Budget Hotel in 1996. In the early stages of our membership of the association, and for a number of years, my uncle of blessed memory, Mr. Ben Ackah-Nyanzu, represented Venaco Lodge at the association's monthly meetings. Upon his death in 2005, I started representing Venaco Lodge at the association's meeting, albeit irregularly, due to my duties at University of Ghana as a lecturer. On occasions that I could not attend, I sent a staff of the Lodge to represent us at the meetings and obliged him/her to present reports of proceedings of the meetings to me. These reports complemented the official minutes of the meetings that I received later.

My attendance at the association's monthly meetings improved substantially when I resigned from the University in 2009. This became possible because my new regime allowed me to devote more time to the Lodge's activities, including those related to the Ghana Hotels Association. Over time I gained a better and clearer understanding of the origin, aims and objectives of the association as well as the several benefits to members.

Ghana Hotels Association (GHA) was formed in 1975 and is made up of Managing Proprietors, Managing Directors or Accredited Representatives of Hotels, Motels, and Guest Houses that have been certified and licensed by the Ghana Tourism Authority (GTA) to offer accommodation, catering and other tourism services in Ghana. Based on GTA categorisation, members have facilities that are certified as budget, guesthouse, or one to five stars. The association has a National Office with eleven (11) branches spread over the ten (10) regions of Ghana and a total membership of over 1,000 members.

The abridged version of the mission of the Association is "to be unified, effective and instrumental in advocating and shaping policies that promote the hotel industry; to provide training and technical assistance to its membership that would strengthen the sector and foster good relationship among members and stakeholders in the tourism industry". The vision of the Association is to see a vibrant hospitality sector whereby all hotels in the country will have qualified/trained personnel who will merit international standards and offer quality service delivery to visitors and to boost tourism to become a leading sector of the Ghanaian economy.

Membership Benefits include:
1. The association provides opportunities for social and business networking among players in the hotel industry.

2. The association serves as a mouthpiece for members and the hotel industry in general, as well as an advocate for improved policies and regulations for the industry.

3. The association negotiates rates for statutory fees such as Business Operating Permit, Fire Certificate Fee, Ghana Tourism Authority Licence Fee, and royalties for use of Audio-Visual works.

4. The association provides opportunities for members to learn more about hotel management practices; and also provides access to information relevant to the hotel industry.

5. The association operates a welfare system which supports members in various ways.

6. The association assists members to deal with challenges that confront their operations.

7. The association provides services to members such as payment of statutory fees, advertising and marketing (hotel directory and website).

8. The association serves as a source of peer pressure for improved services and standards among member hotels.

9. The association provides access to cheap sources of hotel supplies and accessories and also makes it possible for members to buy goods on credit.

Consequently I took a personal decision to contribute my quota to its growth and development through active participation at monthly meetings and prompt payment of our financial obligations. I guess I underestimated the significance of my contribution to the association till I was approached by the National Secretary of the Association, Mrs. Juliet Taylor, to contest the chairmanship of the Greater Accra Regional Branch of the Association. This was in mid 2013 when the chairmanship position was due to be vacant in January 2014. My initial response to Mrs. Taylor was that I wouldn't have the time to perform that role. But Mrs. Taylor persisted so I requested her to give me two weeks to think and pray about it.

In the course of the two weeks whilst I was thinking and praying about Mrs. Taylor's proposal, I received a call from my sister in-law, Dr. (Mrs.) Gwendolyn Bayitse (my wife's sister). During our chat she informed me of a Church programme that she attended with her then boyfriend, Philip (they are happily married now), where the Pastor made some revelations about me. According to her, the Pastor mentioned among other things that God has plans for me in the hospitality business so I should prepare and look forward to that. I received this information from my sister in-law as an answer to my prayers. It further assured me that God answers prayers and influences our decisions and choices if we are prepared to obey Him.

I contested the election against the sitting vice-chairman. My campaign message, which was communicated mainly through text messages and emails, was simple: "to make the Greater Accra Regional Branch of the Ghana Hotels Association more attractive to members, non-members and indeed all stakeholders". On the day of the elections, held at Labadi Beach Hotel, I had the opportunity, as my opponent, to present my plans for the Region and to convince members to vote for me. Suffice to say, my message sunk very well with members and they voted massively for me to win a landslide victory.

Other executive positions voted for on the day were Vice-Chairman, Secretary, Treasurer, and Assistant Treasurer. To set the ball rolling I developed an Operations Manual to guide the work of the executive team which was largely a fresh team. The Operations Manual dealt with issues related to: conduct of executive and general meetings; request, disbursement and retirement of accountable imprest; payment of staff salaries; T&T allowances for meetings; stock taking of secretariat equipment and materials; duties of the secretariat staff; and welfare processing.

To create a sense of commitment and dedication among members for the Greater Accra Regional Branch, I developed a Pledge for the branch which reads as follows: *"I believe in the Ghana Hotels Association so I pledge to make the Accra Branch attractive to all stakeholders and I know together we can make a difference so help me God"*. The pledge is recited at all executive and general meetings of the branch.

Again to guide activities of the branch for a year, I introduced the development of annual programmes which captures brief background and state of the branch, the branch's goals for the year, the activities that need to be undertaken to achieve the goals, calendar of activities, the proposed budget, the principles that guide the implementation of activities and the conditions necessary to achieve the goals. For 2014, 2015 and 2016, the annual programmes were presented to members at general meetings for discussion and approval and then served as a blueprint of activities in the branch for the respective years. The annual programmes have been very instrumental in keeping the branch focused. God willing, I will present my last annual programme in 2017 which will be the end of my four-year term as chairman of the branch in line with the constitution of the Association.

Related to the annual programmes I also introduced the presentation of midyear and annual reports. The annual report contains a brief background of the Greater Accra Regional Branch, a statement by the Branch Chairman, and an outline of the Branch's projected goals for the year and proposed activities as stated in the Branch's Annual Programme for that particular year. This is followed by the actual activities undertaken in the year, as well as the extent to which the projected goals were achieved. The Branch's financial performance in the year is also available in the report. The report ends with some recommendations for the following year. The midyear report followed the same structure as the annual report albeit the focus is on activities undertaken from January to June of the year in question. Where necessary some adjustments were made in the annual programme for the second half of the year based on the midyear report. This is all in line with transparency and accountability which I promised the members of the Association during my acceptance speech as Chairman of the Regional Branch of the Ghana Hotels Association.

By the constitution of the Association the secretary and I represent the branch on the National Executive Council (NEC) of the Association where major decisions and policies concerning the Association are made. Together with eight other members of the branch we also represent the branch at Congress which is the highest decision making body of the Association.

One of my significant achievement as chairman of the branch was the acquisition of a vehicle for the branch. My predecessor had initiated the vehicle acquisition process with the institution of a levy on members. Even though some monies were raised through the vehicle levy it was far inadequate to purchase a vehicle. Based on a suggestion and encouragement by some members of the branch I developed a proposal for sponsorship and distributed to several organisations.

Out of the over hundred sponsorship letters sent out, only two organisations, Unibank and MET Insurance responded positively. Unfortunately discussions with MET Insurance fell through due to some existing legal clauses between the National Office of the Association and other insurance companies. Discussions with Unibank went on till the point where a Memorandum of Understanding (M.O.U) was developed. The M.O.U. was first discussed and unanimously approved at the 30th April 2015 General Meeting of the Branch held at Mövenpick Ambassador Hotel. The M.O.U was then presented to the National Office of the Association and subsequently approved, subject to a few amendments, at the National Executive Council meeting of the Association held on 25th June 2015 at Elmina Beach Resort, Elmina.

Unibank accepted the proposed amendments and the M.O.U. was signed at Korkdam Hotel, Achimota. The vehicle, a 15-Seater Toyota Hiace Minibus was eventually released to the Association by Toyota Company Ghana Ltd on 22nd September 2015 after Unibank had transferred $36,156 (Thirty-six thousand one hundred and fifty six US Dollars) for the payment of the vehicle to Toyota Company Ghana Ltd. The vehicle, with registration number GX1495-15, was subsequently insured (Comprehensive) by the Branch with Star Assurance at an annual premium of Gh4,099.30 (Four Thousand Ninety-Nine Ghana Cedis and Thirty Pesewas).

Representatives of Unibank handed over the vehicle to the Branch at its 21st October 2015 meeting held at Fiesta Royale Hotel. The short but impressive ceremony was graced by the National President and National Secretary of the Association. Unibank was represented by Jerry Afful, Yvonne Kittoe and Della Owusu. I received the key to the vehicle from Della Owusu, head of Business Banking within Corporate Banking, Unibank.

Another significant achievement during my term of office was the preparation and submission of a proposal for the appointment of an Executive Secretary for the Association. At the time of going to press with this book the proposal had been approved by the NEC awaiting further consultations to effect it.

At the end of my first two-year term of office as Chairman of the branch, I received an award at the maiden Ghana Hotels Association Awards as Regional Chairman of the year 2015. Twenty nine other awards were given to various individuals and member hotels at the ceremony which was organised at La Palm Royal Beach Hotel on Saturday 23rd January 2016. As part of activities to publicize the awards programme I featured on the breakfast show of Ghana's national television station, GTV, with Mrs. Juliet Taylor, the National Secretary of the Association. I also wrote a short article on the Award which was published in the Daily Graphic in the morning of Saturday 23rd January 2016.

## 6:3    RECAP OF PERSONAL LEADERSHIP SKILLS, QUALITIES AND TRAITS

Looking back at my leadership experiences under the various circumstances outlined above I can tease out the following as some of the traits and disposition that enabled me to perform my leadership roles effectively.

- I always have an insatiable quest to support groups to grow and develop. This propels me to continually look for ways to support the group and most of the time I find those ways to help. I believe this is born out of general compassion and love for humanity.

- I am very sensitive and passionate about effective communication so I put in a lot of efforts to get it right. This helps me to get my communication right with members of the groups I lead.

- Naturally I respect rules and regulations and I consciously try not to break rules and regulations. I have observed that this trait gives me the confidence to address sensitive issues in groups and places me beyond reproach. It reduces the chances of members disrespecting and working against me.

- Since I reconciled with God and renewed my walk with Him I have developed an attitude of total dependency on Him that empowers me to take bold and daring decisions in the interest of the group. Once I sense that God is on my part on an issue, I spare no effort to push it through. Most of the time I get it right.

- I have a very high sense of integrity which has resulted in a craze for transparency and accountability in my leadership roles. I have observed that the appreciable practice of transparency and accountability grants me the boldness to face people and issues without fear.

- Respect for time. This is one area that has helped me very much in my leadership role. I have absolute respect for time and over the years I have been able to resist the temptation of being corrupted by the popular "Ghana Man Time" where appointments are delayed one to three hours beyond the official time.

You receive an invitation to attend a meeting at 3pm and the meeting gets started at 5pm with the usual "we apologise for the late start of the meeting; it was due to circumstances beyond our control". I put in a lot of effort, a lot of the times to my discomfort, to attend programmes on time and I have actually created a good time-image for myself. The benefit is that people take me seriously.

- I improve myself regularly through self-assessment and self-development efforts. I read and write a lot all in an attempt to improve myself. I assess where I fall short in my leadership role and try to study to improve upon that area. I hold a principle that I can study and understand anything that I want to know and this has helped me tremendously. The advent of the internet and ease of search for knowledge through various search engines has made such self-education much more accessible and easier.

- Ever since I perceived planning, implementation, monitoring and evaluation as the basic functions of a leader I have adhered to them and use them in all leadership roles that I play. It puts everything in perspective and gives me absolute control over everything that I do as a leader. Now I do not see how I can lead without planning, implementation, monitoring and evaluation.

- An attitude that I believe has inspired me a lot in my various leadership roles is the fact that I respect and attach seriousness to every leadership role that play. If I cannot perform a leadership role for whatever reason, I make sure I do not accept it neither do I allow myself to be coerced to accept it. But once I accept to do it then I take it with all seriousness. So the seriousness that I attach to my role as Convenor of APSU 84 is the same seriousness that I attach to my role as Chairman of Greater Accra Regional Branch of Ghana Hotels Association. The respect that I attached to my role as head of Department of Agricultural Extension, University of Ghana Legon, is the same respect that I give to my role as head of Ackah-Nyamike Jnr. family. Bottom line is that all leadership roles, no matter how small or big deserve a leaders respect and serious attention.

- Once I take up a leadership position, I cannot help but think about the role all the time. As the saying goes, "I eat it, drink it, sleep it, dream it" etc. I constantly try to figure out what to do to inspire, grow and develop the group. I contemplate a lot of strategies and ideas and discuss them regularly with those close to me. My wife is usually at the receiving end of this because I bombard her regularly with my thoughts and plans. The benefit of this posture is that I am never short of plans and ideas for a group and it also allows me to venture into the preferred future of the group and how to get the group there. Some call it visionary but I simply refer to it as thinking into the future.

- My humility and unassuming posture has also been very helpful. I consciously show respect to everybody I encounter in the course of my leadership role irrespective of their social, economic or political standing. I prefer to focus on the Spirit of God in every individual and that helps me to respect them accordingly irrespective of their shortfalls. I must mention that my humility does not make me weak or easy walk over for people. Indeed I demonstrate firmness in my convictions and change my mind only when I am convinced otherwise.

- Over the years I have also developed a 'listening ear' that enables me to focus on the thoughts of others rather than focus only on what I have to offer. I also learnt that too many interjections interfere with people's effort to develop genuine and helpful arguments. Thus the less the interjections, the more the possibility of picking some sound ideas from a chat. Apart from enabling me to understand things from other perspectives, it also motivates people to contribute to discussions and make proposals which they would ordinarily not make. This attribute helps a lot in my chairing of meetings as a leader.

The above attributes and many more not listed here continue to enable me excel as a leader.

# EPILOGUE

I have attempted in this book to demystify leadership and thereby make it easy to understand and practice. My attempts included an exposition of what leadership is all about, the functions of a leader, the benefits of effective leadership and what a leader needs to perform effectively. To put the expositions in perspective I shared my leadership experiences and rounded it up with an outline of my leadership skills, traits and qualities.

Much as I perceive a substantial component of my leadership traits and qualities as natural, I also believe that leadership can be learnt and effective leadership is possible, requiring a conscious effort to learn and practice skills and attitudes that empowers a leader to guide, support and inspire a group to address their needs, problems and aspirations.

Leadership is also versatile as the title of the book and my leadership experiences suggests. In other words, once a person learns the leadership trade, he can apply it to various roles that require him to guide, support and inspire people to address their needs, problems and aspirations.

You can lead, so take up that mantle and lead effectively.